SECOND MARRIAGE

AN INSIDER'S GUIDE TO HOPE, HEALING & LOVE

SHARILEE SWAITY

ENDORSEMENTS

In a world where marriages come and go, and where there are caring people struggling to make a go of a second or third marriage, Sharilee's book is a breath of fresh air and a source of hope and a future. No remarried husband or wife or stepchild can afford to miss reading this book, reflecting on its guidance and growing through its application.

--Alex Cross, pastor at Wayside Gospel Chapel

Through a combination of research and personal experience, Sharilee has provided a map for those walking a road filled with ups and downs. She gives us topics for discussion and issues that may need to be addressed in each couple's particular situation. This is not a book with all the answers, but a guidebook for the different ways a couple can find themselves on this new road in life.

-- Edee Frank, M.R.S, Counseling, Counselling Therapist

For information about special discounts available for bulk purchases or review copies, please contact the publisher at admin@secondmarriage.xyz.

For more materials on the subject outlined in this book, visit the author's website http://secondmarriage.xyz.

Book editing by Paula Pietrobono.

All Scriptures are from the King James Version of the Bible, which is in the public domain.

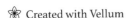 Created with Vellum

This book is dedicated to my gorgeous husband, Vernon Neil Swaity. You are my warrior, my lover, my entertainer, and my fixer. I love you and am blessed to be your wife. Thank you for asking me to dance nine years ago and for never giving up on us. I look forward to the next nine years with pleasure. It just keeps getting better!

Thank you for helping me find my dreams again. Seven years ago, you were the one who whispered to me late at night, "Why don't you write?" "Really?" I answered anxiously, afraid that it was just a frivolous pastime. "Yes, see where it goes," you told me.

You are the kindest, most generous, hardest working man I have ever met. I am honoured to stand beside you as your woman and your friend. Thank you for inviting me into your family to be a stepmom to your two wonderful sons.

ACKNOWLEDGMENTS

Thank you to the Lord Jesus Christ for saving me and giving me hope. Without You, O Lord, I could do nothing.

Thank you to my editor, Paula Pietrobono, who also happens to be my sister. Your eye for detail and the right turn of phrase is amazing.

Thank you to the beautiful women and men who agreed to share their stories with me for this book. You have inspired me to make my marriage better.

Thank you to the church family that took us in and accepted us, with all our imperfections. Your support has meant so much.

Thank you to the marriage counsellor who helped save our marriage.

TABLE OF CONTENTS

ABOUT THIS BOOK

 A room without books is like a body without a soul.

— CICERO

My husband, Vern and I, have been married for nine years now. For the first four years, we weren't sure if we would survive as a couple but through prayer, counselling and hard work, we can now say that we are "happily married."

To make it work, we have both had to overcome the major baggage we brought into our relationship. We are both people who like to help and in many ways, we tried to "rescue" each other. Unfortunately, rescuing each other almost led to both of us drowning.

I started writing on this topic seven years ago with a simple little article[1] designed to encourage others who might be struggling like we were, and was surprised by how many people were looking for help. I am not a psychologist but have a keen interest in human relationships and in helping those who are hurting.

In this book, I share some very personal stories about our marriage and I want to stress that I do so with full permission from my husband. He is just as passionate as I am about helping struggling couples.

In addition to our own narrative, I will also share the stories of three couples who trusted me enough to bare their souls and lives to the world. Their names and details have been changed to protect their privacy but their stories are still true. I think you will relate to much of what they have to share.

WHAT YOU WILL GET

This book is for people who are struggling in their second marriage. Chapter by chapter, I address many of the issues people have in a remarriage situation, such as healing from the past, personality differences and connecting with stepchildren.

The following is a list of what you will gain from the book, *Second Marriage: An Insider's Guide to Hope, Healing and Love*:

- A better understanding of why second marriage is so difficult
- Powerful strategies for letting go of your past
- Knowledge about how both sex and friendship are the keys to romance
- An approach to how to deal with personality differences
- Help in connecting with your stepchildren

WHO THIS BOOK IS FOR

- The main audience for this book are people who have been married more than once, and their partners.
- It is written for both men and women -- gender pronouns are alternated throughout the book.
- Stepfamilies who weren't married before but have children from a previous relationship and are dealing with stepfamily issues.
- Those involved in serving people in second marriages, such as therapists and ministers.
- Those considering a second marriage and wanting to know what to expect.

THE EXERCISES

I would love to offer you a beautiful gift to help you work through these exercises. It is a fully interactive PDF workbook that you can get, for free, at: http://secondmarriage.xyz/sign-free-resources-page/.

In all the chapters, you will find exercises or reflection questions that are designed to help you put the strategies in the book into practice in your own life. They will also help you reflect on your own life.

PROLOGUE: NEVER GONNA DANCE AGAIN

*W*hen my first husband left me for another woman, I thought I would never love again. My mother told me that loving someone new would make me forget the pain. She was right.

It took a while, though. Ten years and two failed relationships later, I finally found "the one." He had been married before, too. We had that in common. We understood each other's broken past but that did not make it easy. We struggled to make it work.

Those of us who lose a marriage, lose a dream. After the dream dies, we don't think we will ever dance again. Until slowly, we awaken and wonder ... maybe?

And we make that brave decision to try again. We are no longer young. Ghosts from the past haunt us.

But we venture on the floor and before we know it, we are dancing again. This book is for all those who thought they would never dance again but found the courage to get up and swing.

Maybe no one told you it would be harder the second time. Everything feels so complicated. You wonder, is this really worth it? This book is born out of the struggles. This book is for you. The complications are many. It isn't the same as the first time. But you have been given a fresh start. May you both dance as you have never danced before.

I

THE DECISION TO MARRY AGAIN

When we first lose our spouse, many of us are initially very reluctant to ever go down the aisle again. But then something changes and we find ourselves part of a "Mr. and Mrs." once more. After we have been married for a while, and the problems are piling up, we may start to question our decision and need to be reminded of why we got married in the first place.

1

WE DON'T WANT TO MARRY AGAIN BUT...

““ Marriage is the triumph of imagination over intelligence. Second marriage is the triumph of hope over experience.

— OSCAR WILDE

*A*fter my divorce at age 22, I stayed single for a long time. I was having fun and not interested in settling down again. That was on the outside. On the inside, however, I knew I could never bear the agony of going through a divorce again.

One evening a group of my colleagues had gone out for dinner. As the desserts came to the table, the subject of marriage came up. Two of us at the table were divorced: my boss and me. "Do you think you guys will ever tie the knot

5

again?" someone asked us. The two of us both shook our heads emphatically, "No, never again!"

At the time, I meant it. After my marriage broke up, I couldn't see myself doing it again. No matter how difficult my marriage got, I had been determined to stick with it. When he walked out the door and never came back, I cried every night for months.

Many years later, I met my next husband-to-be. By then, I thought I was ready. I had finally met a nice guy. When we started to get serious, I brought up the idea of a wedding ring. His exact response was "marriage sucks," and "I hate marriage – yuck." He wanted no part of matrimony because he wanted no part of divorce. Once had been enough.

That decision to walk down the aisle again is rarely an easy one to make for those of us who have already lost a spouse. A 2006 study conducted by Statistics Canada showed that *only* 22% of divorced individuals were positive about wanting to marry again, while 78% said they either did not want to remarry or they were unsure.[1]

NEVER AGAIN?

Can you remember back when you lost your spouse, to either divorce or bereavement? Did you think you would ever marry again? If not, what changed your mind?

Our first interview couple, Angus and Betty Jones share their experiences with me. Angus is a tall man in his late fifties who works as a high school principal. He loves to meet new people and seems like the last person who would struggle with confidence. Immediately following his second divorce at the age of 40, he said this about remarriage: "Never again! I told myself that if I ever got married again, this time it would be for money. She could take care of me! I didn't want to do it again. It was just too painful."

Angus had no desire to try something again that had failed not just once, but twice for him. These feelings are common for those who have gone through losing their marriage but like many of us, something changed his mind. In the case of Angus, the "something" that changed his mind was named Betty.

When they met, Betty was a classy, 32-year-old kindergarten teacher. Although they were both educators, they worked in different school districts. They first noticed each other at a community event, where Angus would go on Saturday nights to listen to jazz. One night, she asked him to go for dinner and offered to pay for herself. Angus was smitten.

Despite Angus's resolve to never get married again, his stance started to soften. They claimed to be "just friends" until Betty was offered a job in another city. Angus knew he had to decide.

"We started off as friends and it was really nice. We just chugged along for months as friends and I didn't want to take it to the next level. I didn't want to lose her as a friend," he explains.

But when Angus realized that Betty might walk out of his life forever, he decided to make a move. He recalls, "We were standing on a bridge together and I leaned over and kissed her. We walked away holding hands. After that, our love grew like a small seed."

MAYBE AGAIN?

Only a small percentage of divorced individuals say they want to try again, but like Angus, most of us eventually do. According to a report called *"Reinvestigating Remarriage: Another Decade of Progress,"* 75% of people who are divorced eventually marry again.[2]

The statistics are similar for those who have lost a spouse to either death or divorce. A 2014 study from Pew Research estimated that approximately six out of ten individuals who were previously married (whether divorced or widowed) eventually remarry.[3]

These statistics are very interesting. It is notable that only about 20% of divorced people say they want to remarry when they first break up but then 75% end up doing so.

Obviously, something is changing their mind about marriage and giving them the confidence to walk down the aisle, again. It is also possible that the people getting married again are doing so, in spite of some reservations, and this is part of their struggle.

Thinking back, if you were unsure about getting remarried when you first lost your spouse, what was it that changed your mind? Is there still a part of you that lacks confidence in your decision? The more you are able to resolve any ambiguity, the more you will be fully present in your new marriage.

REFLECTION QUESTIONS

The following questions are for those who were previously married. If you were not married before, ask these questions of your spouse.

. . .

1. IMMEDIATELY AFTER LOSING YOUR FIRST SPOUSE, WHICH OF THE following best described your feelings about getting remarried?

    a. Never again!

    b. Probably not

    c. Maybe someday

    d. I hope so

    e. I am ready

2. HOW LONG AFTER YOUR BEREAVEMENT OR DIVORCE DID YOU start to consider marrying again?

    a. Ten years plus

    b. 5-10 years

    c. 1-5 years

    d. Less than one year

3. ON A SCALE OF 1-5, HOW READY DO YOU THINK YOU WERE TO remarry when you walked down the aisle?

    1 2 3 4 5

MOST OF US REMARRY QUICKLY

> Keep your eyes wide open before marriage, half
> shut afterwards.

— BENJAMIN FRANKLIN

Many people rush into second marriage. Think back to your decision to walk down the aisle again. Were you truly ready?

Many of us aren't ready but we do it anyway. The reasons why are understandable. We are hurting and lonely and another chance at love beckons us. But sometimes we make our hurt worse. There is still hope, though, when we reconnect with the dreams that motivated us to marry and the part of us that wanted another chance at love.

Elise and Alex are our next interview couple. They are a vibrant couple in their early 40's who have been married for ten years. Alex is constantly on the move and loves his job as a small restaurant manager. Elise works part-time as a home care worker quietly helping seniors with their day-to-day needs.

When the two of them first met at their local church, Alex was immediately smitten. She definitely was not. She'd been alone for ten years and wasn't looking for anyone. Alex was freshly divorced.

Elise says, "He told me it was love at first sight. When he saw me worshipping at church, he wanted to marry me." Alex proposed six months later and they were married within a year.

Elise and Alex's quick marriage is typical of second-marriage couples. A review of research done in 2000 found that almost one third of divorced individuals got married within one year and that number peaks at *one only month* after the papers go through. The same report said that of those left widowed, there are many who marry within 13 months of being widowed.[1]

The *Reinvestigating Remarriage* report also found that many couples are living together within a few months of starting a relationship. In this case, the relationship is starting even earlier but without a solid commitment. When a couple moves in together so quickly they are not giving themselves time to get to know each other first, before the very real pressures of a relationship begin.

Like so many second-married couples, my husband and I were quick to jump into a relationship after we had just met. Because of this, we did not give ourselves enough time to get to know each other and plan out the complicated issues to come.

In the next section, I will share our pre-marriage dating

story. We messed up a lot of things but I hope others can learn from our mistakes. Our story shows there is hope for all of us.

OUR MOVED-WAY-TOO-FAST DATING STORY

My husband and I met in the most modern of ways: through an online dating site. I was working as a teacher up in Northern Canada and he lived over 1000 miles away in Winnipeg, Manitoba.

I had been burned before and was very nervous at the thought of meeting, never mind dating, anyone new. He had also been hurt deeply and was very cautious. When we started communicating, though, all of that caution was thrown out the window. Before even hearing his voice, I was smitten by his flirty, funny messages. A week after our first message, he asked for my phone number and we talked all night.

After a couple of weeks of talking on the phone, I wanted to marry him. I felt a peace about him I had never felt before. He made me feel comfortable and safe.

Two months later, he took a plane to where I was staying and helped me move across the country. I loved the way he took charge and helped me however he could. When our vehicle started having mechanical problems, he dug in and tried to fix it himself. We travelled across three provinces. It was an adventure.

When we got to the city, I started looking for a place to live and a job. In the meantime, I stayed at his mom and sister's house. He had just started staying there, too, trying to reconnect with a family he had never known. Unable to find full-time work in my field, the stay lasted longer than I intended. Nine months later, I was still there and we were fighting constantly.

We were near strangers living in the same house, trying to figure out a new relationship. We were living with his family, whom even he didn't know that well. He started drinking heavily. I was on edge and hard to live with.

After nine months, I packed my bags and moved out one night while he was gone to a party. I stayed with a friend for two weeks and then booked a hotel room to live in because it was all I could afford. What a fall -- from being a high school teacher living in a beautiful condo to living in a hotel, working at a call centre. I felt depressed and hopeless.

For six months, we did not talk to one another but he was still on my mind. I saved my money and got myself an apartment and was starting to get my life together, when he called. He asked for forgiveness and genuinely listened when I told him how angry I was. It truly seemed like we were both changed people and we quickly rekindled our relationship. Two months later, he asked me to marry him and we were married three months later.

The way we started our relationship led to problems. We got together too quickly and we were so focused on sorting out our own conflicts that we did not discuss how to handle the upcoming complications: finances and forming a new family. As well, we both still had a severe lack of trust from previous relationships. All of this came out in those first years of marriage.

HOPE FOR A BAD BEGINNING

I share this time of our life with you to encourage you. No matter what your beginnings were, it is never too late to learn from them. Like many couples getting remarried, my husband and I forged right into the fire and learned things the hard way. We thought we had healed from our past, but our behaviour showed that we still needed deep healing.

Looking back, more time spent planning our future would have helped but we didn't realize how important that was. I want to encourage you that if you also married in haste, it is not too late to make things better now.

Despite the mistakes we made, however, our hearts were in the right place. We really did want to love each other. We had a desire to make each other's lives better. We hoped that we would be able to form a loving family together.

To end this chapter, I want to remind you that you got married for a reason. Even if your marriage seems like one big mess, go back and examine the reasons that you originally got married.

Was it for a second chance at love? Did you hope to have another opportunity for happiness? Did you dream of forging a new family unit? Most of us must have believed that our upcoming marriage would be a culmination of some of our dreams: perhaps happiness, love, a family. Do any of these hopes and dreams resonate with you?

- You hoped your life would get better.
- You hoped your children would love your new spouse.
- You hoped your new spouse would understand you.

- You hoped that you would have a happy marriage.
- You hoped you would forget the past.

Most of us have dreams and hopes when we enter marriage the second time but when things go awry, we forget why we ever married in the first place. The following powerful exercise will help you reconnect with your reasons for getting married.

After we have been married for a while, we sometimes take it for granted and forget that we were searching for something. We needed someone. We were not complete on our own.

"MY HOPES AND DREAMS" EXERCISE

Think back to when you were considering marriage to your current spouse. What were you hoping for? Another way of wording this is, what were you looking for?

POINTERS

- It may have been something you didn't think about consciously.
- It could have been something general, such as happiness, or perhaps something specific, such as a partner to share your jokes with.
- Be honest about your desires. Don't censor yourself out of embarrassment.

Here are some examples to get you started:

- You hoped for a happy marriage
- You wanted everyone to be a family
- You wanted a companion to share life with
- You desired sexual fulfillment
- You wanted to share life with your best friend
- You wanted an exciting life
- You wanted someone who would share your hobbies

These are just a few examples; yours will be unique to your life and personality. The reason for doing this exercise is to get back in touch with the real reasons that you got married. Then, when you feel like giving up on your marriage, take a look at the desires that drew you to wanting to spend the rest of your life with your spouse and remind yourself of how much fuller your life is, with your spouse, in spite of the problems!

I. FILL OUT THE FOLLOWING EXERCISE, WITH A MINIMUM OF three statements:

I was hoping for ...

II

SECOND MARRIAGE
CHALLENGES

This section is to help understand what makes second marriages so complicated: both the circumstances and the emotions we bring to the table.

3

WHY ARE THINGS SO COMPLICATED?

 The course of true love never did run smooth.

— WILLIAM SHAKESPEARE

*H*ave you ever seen someone use the "complicated" option for their Facebook profile page and wondered what their situation was? Well, if you are in a second marriage, you could probably tick the "complicated" box on your status and it would be accurate. (But don't to that, because complicated on Facebook really means non-committed!)

Dr. Ron J. Hammond, in his book, Sociology of the Family, states that "Stepfamilies may well be the most complicated family systems on the planet." Hammond then goes on to recognize that stepfamilies and remarried couples can be "emotionally battle-worn" from all of the complication.[1] What is it about second marriage that can make it so complicated? These next two chapters will explain.

THE FORMER SPOUSE

First of all, in a second marriage, one or both of you have been married to someone else and that is something that couples in a first marriage do not have to contend with. There are three possibilities for a former spouse in a second marriage.

The Former Spouse of the Widowed

The first scenario for a second marriage is that one or both of the partners is widowed. The former spouse is no longer on this earth but can still play a role in the remarriage through memories. A new spouse may feel like he is competing with a memory.

Betty Jones had never married her former boyfriend but the memory of her former suitor still played a part in their marriage. Angus explains that even twenty-five years later, he sometimes feels like he can't compete:

> *I still feel that because Jordan died, he was taken away from her and I wonder if he is going to meet her on the other side. Will he be waiting for her after death? Maybe I am with her just while we are here on earth.*

A widower might feel guilt about moving on with someone else. In the movie, *We Bought a Zoo,*[2] Matt Damon plays a newly widowed character named Benjamin Mee who has a line of single women offering to help the distressed widower with fancy-looking casseroles. Mee shows no interest in the band of sweet women coming to his rescue because he is still grieving the loss of his late wife.

When he buys a zoo, however, he and the main zookeeper, played by Scarlett Johannsen, start to become dangerously close and Benjamin shuts her out, terrified that if he lets her in, he will be betraying the love of his life. She finally convinces him that his wife would have wanted him to continue living.

Divorced with no Kids

The second possible scenario is when two people were married but they did not have any children together. In this case, there may still be lingering effects from grieving the marriage but in most cases, there is no reason to have to keep seeing the former spouse.

This was the case for my former husband and me. After our divorce was finalized, we only talked one or two times in total and then both went our separate ways. This situation is by far the least complicated of second marriage possibilities but it still means that the individual must cope with healing from the past.

Divorced with Children

Finally, the most complex situation is when one or both of the partners have had children with their former spouse. In this case, unless the children are all grown up, that ex is now permanently part of the marriage. This is my husband's situation. He and his ex-wife had two sons before they were divorced.

The other spouse will always be a part of the couple's life and will have a direct impact on the schedule and lifestyle of the new couple. If the ex-spouse decides to go to court and requests a change in custody, their life can be turned upside down in a heartbeat. The individuals within the relationship must decide how to deal with this person who is now a permanent third wheel in their relationship.

THE CHILDREN

Second marriages often have children from the first marriage(s), and this is never simple. Bringing these little lives into the mix means that the marriage is not just two people getting married.

It is three, four or more people getting married, and bringing all your lives together. The adjustments and changes are extensive and there is no painless way around them. Take the adjustment of a newly married couple with no kids and magnify that many times over: that is the adjustment required for a second marriage with kids.

The young married couple can dream of children sometime in the distant future but second-marriagers with children do not have this luxury. The needs of the children do not go on hold while the two of you have a honeymoon and get to know each other. Even if you don't have full-time custody, the children will always be on your mind.

So, to conclude, when you are dealing with children, it means that you are not just meeting each other's needs; you are meeting the needs of the children while also learning to adjust to each other. When the baby comes *after* the wedding, couples have time to get used to each other before the pressure of children. In a blended family, the children are already there and the "becoming a family" thing happens all at once.

THE COURTS AND GOVERNMENT

Another factor that can make remarriage more complicated is the possible presence of the courts and government in your life. Because custody and support payments are dictated by the court and enforced through a government department, an outside body has a big say in what happens in your life.

The courts can determine several things in your life, including your schedule for having the children, where you can live and even where you can travel. This takes away the autonomy of the couple and hands it to an impersonal governing body.

THE MONEY SITUATION IS COMPLEX

The financial situation for second marriages can be quite complicated. First, for many there may have been an expensive divorce. Going through the court system is rarely cheap and often can cripple someone's financial situation. Child support also greatly complicates the financial situation of a remarried couple.

When my husband and I first got married, we bought a small, inexpensive mobile home to save on costs. When we went to sell it, however, it was hard to get rid of. After a couple of unsuccessful attempts with realtors, we decided to sell it on our own.

As people came to view the home, we noticed a strange phenomenon. Almost all the potential candidates were divorced men. It seems like they were the only ones willing to live in such a modest home and they were the ones who were the most broke.

REFLECTION QUESTIONS

1. Look at this list of possible complicating circumstances, and check off the ones that apply to your situation:

    a. An ex-spouse

    b. Children

    c. Courts and Government

    d. Money complications

    How many of these apply to you? Remember that the more complications, the harder it is to adjust!

2. OUT OF THE LIST OF POSSIBLE FACTORS COMPLICATING YOUR marriage, which has been the most challenging for you personally?

4

COMPLICATED EMOTIONS

66 If I have lost confidence in myself, I have the
universe against me.

— RALPH WALDO EMERSON

*C*ircumstances are not the only things that make
second marriages complicated. The complication
also comes from inside, from our emotions. On one hand, we
are excited to be starting our new life together but on the other
hand, we may still be suffering from the residue of our past
marriage or other relationships. One part of us is looking
forward to the future while another part is terrified of not
making it.

You may wonder if mixed emotions are a sign that your
marriage is not working but please be assured these
complicated feelings are normal.

EXCITED BUT JADED

People in a second marriage may feel like everything has been done before. We (or our spouse) have had married sex before. We were called Mr. or Mrs. something. We may have signed mortgage papers with someone else.

So, no matter how excited we are to accomplish something together, there may also be the lingering memories of having done this already, and the temptation is to compare our lives now to our lives then. We try our best not to compare, but it can happen without meaning to.

As a spouse of a remarried person, we may feel a bit sad that we were not their first. At whatever it is. Every time you go to do something new as a couple, you wonder if your spouse is reminded of their past. In Chapter 11, I will give you an exercise to help you to accept your story, with all its imperfections.

PASSIONATE BUT INSECURE

The knowledge that our spouse has experienced married life before can lead us to the next set of mixed emotions: passionate but insecure. In fact, the more passion you feel for your spouse, the more insecure you may feel. The reason for this is that when we feel highly attached, it can also lead to feeling vulnerable and that vulnerability can make us scared of losing that person.

There is an episode on the television show, *Heartland*, where one of the characters, Lou, is getting married to a divorced man, but it is *her* first wedding. Throughout the episode, she becomes more and more determined to track down information about her fiancé's previous wedding. She wanted to know details such as where the ceremony was held and how many guests attended.

She pesters him endlessly until he finally shouts out, "Yes, I was married before. There's nothing I can do but you have to stop obsessing about it." In hilarious fashion, she refuses to listen to his advice and continues to fret about it, and eventually researches her perceived competitor online. [1]

The episode is funny because there is so much truth to it. Sometimes it is hard not to compare ourselves to the other person that our spouse was married to, no matter how passionate the two of *us* are together. In Chapter 10, we will talk more about dealing with insecurity.

At other times, our insecurity stems not from our spouse's past but our own. If we were cheated on, abandoned, rejected or abused, the ability to fully trust another human being in such an intimate relationship as marriage seems unrealistic.

As passionate as we may feel about this new person who has promised to love and protect us, we feel bound with mistrust and suspicion. It is not even a conscious thought but rather a constant oppression. Every little look, any little discrepancy can be a trigger for wondering if we can trust our current partner.

HOPEFUL BUT BROKEN

Mark is an athletic man in his forties who works as a welder. He gives off a confident demeanour and is quick to crack a joke. He talks about what he brought into his second marriage:

 My confidence was affected. My ex told me that I was

a terrible husband, and that affects me in this marriage.

When Mark and his wife have a conflict, he immediately thinks he is doing a bad job and finds it very difficult to take any feedback. Even though Mark is hopeful about their future together, he has lost the easy confidence of youth.

The reality is, going through a divorce breaks us and we are not the same people we were before it happened. If you are widowed, your world also fell apart. No matter how hopeful we are now, we may still be hurting from our past.

COMMITTED BUT FEELING GUILTY

Another emotion that can wreak havoc with those in a second marriage is guilt. Even though we are committed to this marriage, we still feel guilty that we were not able to make the last one work. This can be the case, especially for people who never wanted the divorce. When things go wrong, we can start thinking that maybe we should not have married again.

Parents often feel guilty about not being able to keep the family together for the sake of their children. Sometimes that guilt can lead to spoiling the children, to make up for their loss. And this guilt can make it hard for people to fully open their heart to this relationship, even though they are determined to stay together.

SURROUNDED BY PEOPLE BUT LONELY

It is ironic that even though we marry for companionship, a second marriage can make us lonelier than we were before.

We may be surrounded by people but not connected to those around us. This is particularly true when a stepfamily has been formed. Stepfamilies can be lonely places because they are often so divided, especially at the beginning.

The stepparent can feel distance from the stepchildren because they don't know each other yet. To the child, the stepparent is often an intruder. Stepchildren often feel lonely because they are missing the parent whom they are not living with.

The biological parent and child(ren) may be grieving the end of the exclusive relationship they enjoyed with their children, as a single-parent household. Before this third party came along, they were alone together, with one parent taking care of everything. The kids may miss the feeling of exclusive access they had to their parent before the other adult came into the household. We will talk more about loneliness in Chapter 20.

LOVING BUT ANGRY

The last set of emotions we will examine regarding remarriage is anger. Even though we love our mate very much, we may feel angry but not know why. If this is the case, there is a good chance it is displaced anger. We aren't truly angry with our spouse but our past is spilling into our present relationship.

Expressing anger in the present, even if it is caused by the past, can bring harm to those around us. Even if we know intellectually that the anger is really directed at someone else, our spouse and family are still hurt by it. In the chapters ahead, we will focus extensively on learning to let go of issues from the past.

REFLECTION QUESTIONS

If you have been struggling with your second or third marriage but were not sure why it was so difficult, I hope these last two chapters made it clearer. No wonder we feel overwhelmed sometimes. Don't give up, though! The good news is that by understanding it and working on it, we can have an even stronger marriage than we thought possible.

1. LOOK AT THIS LIST OF EMOTIONS. WHICH ONES (IF ANY) APPLY to you? Which ones apply to your spouse?

    a. Jaded

    b. Insecure

    c. Broken

    d. Feeling guilty

    e. Lonely

2. OUT OF THIS LIST OF COMPLICATED EMOTIONS, WHICH HAS been the most challenging for you, personally?

3. OUT OF THIS LIST OF COMPLICATED EMOTIONS, WHICH DO YOU think has been most challenging for your spouse?

III

HEALING FROM YOUR PAST

This next part is one of the longest sections of the whole book. Many people in second marriages *think* they are over their past but really, it haunts them, even if they don't talk about it. In this section, we delve deeply into why we are still affected by the past and how we can overcome the issues that weigh us down. We talk about forgiveness and accountability, and then acceptance.

5

GETTING A NEW PERSPECTIVE

66 We can complain because the roses have thorns
or rejoice that the thorns have roses.

— ABRAHAM LINCOLN

So, how are you doing? Did you find that list of complications overwhelming? Does it make you feel determined to overcome or want to retreat under a blanket and hide from the world? It's good to know the truth, but when we consider what we are dealing with, it can be quite daunting. We need to have hope. This next chapter will examine the importance of perspective and encourage you to get a new view of your situation, despite the messiness!

My husband and I live close to a large lake and one of my favourite ways to start the day is to photograph the sun as it rises across the lake. What is amazing to me is how a different perspective of the exact same scene results in such a completely different picture

By focusing mostly on the sky, the sky itself becomes what people notice. In other photos, I like to bow down low, and get a closer look at the ground, with the sky in the distance as background, and the water becomes the focus.

This reminds me of the fact that how we view of our marital situation has a big effect on our results. If we focus on what we don't have, it will seem worse and worse. If we focus more on what we do have, things can start to seem better and better. This chapter is about learning to get our focus off the things we *don't* have, and more on the things we *do* have.

WE DREAM OF MARRIAGE

I want you to think back to when you were a teenager. Did you dream about marriage? Did you have an ideal in your mind about the person you would end up with? Women more than men anticipate our wedding date with great expectation. We are brought up to believe that weddings are magical and that marriage will be our happily ever after.

None of our childhood fantasies ever involved being married a *second time*. When we dream of marriage, it is a dream of having our *own* children, with just *one* spouse forever after. We dream of growing old with that person and of telling our grandchildren our love story.

But then ... that first marriage's end was nothing like we dreamed. That wonderful picture we had of our lives together, with one person forever and ever is broken. That was not how it was supposed to be!

We didn't dream of custody battles, taking care of someone

else's children, or being betrayed by someone who said they would love us forever. We didn't secretly wish for stepkids hating us, financial struggles or the pain of seeing our children's lives fall apart. In the case of the widowed, we believed we would grow old with our spouse, not have to watch them die. We never imagined a funeral instead of a retirement together.

As an idealist, this was something I really had to wrestle with myself. Inside, I protested, "But *it's not supposed to be this way!*" And I was right. It isn't supposed to be this way. Couples are supposed to stay married. Families are supposed to stay together. Hearts are not supposed to be broken but they are.

WE LIVE IN A BROKEN WORLD

Unfortunately, we live in a fallen world and reality is often far from ideal. This is true for both first and second marriages but it just seems more obvious when we are remarried. It's always easy to look at other people's lives and think their lives are better. Let's try to get a different perspective, though.

Even if we had stayed married to one person for life, it is guaranteed there would have been problems. There still would have been pain and heartache and disappointment. The two of you would have probably fought and perhaps wondered why you were together. Life happens to all of us, divorced, single or married.

In fact, whether it is our first marriage or our third one, the ideals and expectations that we bring to marriage can actually cause us to be dissatisfied when we are expecting something that isn't even possible. When we expect our spouse to be perfect and always nice and always attentive to our needs, we are sure to be disappointed. Whatever ideal we had in our mind was probably very unrealistic in the first place, likely impossible.

COMING TO TERMS WITH REALITY

Coming to terms with a less than ideal reality was something 32-year-old Betty had to wrestle with before making her decision to marry Angus. Before Betty met him, the kindergarten teacher had been engaged to another man who had passed away. Losing her first love was devastating enough but marrying a man who had been married not once but twice, seemed almost too much to bear.

This situation was far from the ideal of which she had dreamed. Friends and family questioned what she was doing.

> *Here I was going out with this guy, kind of rough and he had three kids. Friends and family were asking, "what are you getting yourself into?"*

Her sister had married into a blended family and she had seen how hard it was for her. It took Betty quite a while to make the decision to become Mrs. Jones but twenty-five years later, her marriage has stood the test of time.

Do you ever find yourself lamenting, "This isn't how it's supposed to be!" If so, what can you do? You need to come to terms with the fact that the perfect ideal in your mind never would have been perfect, anyway.

This is a fallen world with fallen people. People are free to make choices that we don't like. Sometimes those choices involve divorcing us, cheating on us, abusing us. People die on us and leave us alone. We grieve all those losses. Besides the terrible tragedies, there are the mundane disappointments of life: money issues, getting old and kids who don't obey us.

Part of healing is to learn to look at things differently. Look at what you *do have* instead of what you *don't have.* For example, look at how wonderful your husband *is* instead of what he *isn't.* Be grateful.

Being thankful for what you have might sound simplistic but it is truly profound. When we learn to accept reality, it doesn't make it all better, all at once. It doesn't mean that we don't still feel depressed or sad sometimes about the disappointments of our life. Sometimes it just means that sadness and gratefulness can coexist, and thankfulness is a little seed that resides in our heart amidst the hurt, a promise of hope again and of a new life. Here are some examples:

- No, I was not fortunate enough to stay with the first man that I married but I am blessed enough to find a man that I fully trust now.
- No, I did not have my own children but I have special children in my life that I am privileged to help raise and get to know.
- I am not wealthy but I have everything I need: a home, food to eat and a car to drive.

THE MOSAIC OF OUR LIVES

I want to share one more story to help illustrate this point. While I was teaching at an alternative high school, I got the students involved in making a mosaic. I got permission to repurpose an old table that was just sitting around. I went to an art supply store for educators and obtained a trunk load of floor tiles, all varied colours and materials, for free.

To prepare to make the table, the male students had a fantastic time breaking down these tiles by throwing them violently against the ground: turning them into a large pile of smaller pieces in all different shapes.

Finally, we used mortar to glue these smaller tile pieces onto the table in interesting patterns. The students loved it. The activity calmed down the louder kids and gave the artistic students an outlet for self-expression. Doing the table as a class brought everyone together.

A mosaic is created by putting together hundreds of little broken pieces from what was once whole. If the artist (or artists, in our case) was to keep yearning after the tiles, or vases that were once whole, he could never concentrate on the new mosaic art piece forming in front of him. So, it is with *our* lives in second marriages.

When we keep longing after the pieces that are broken and wishing they were still whole, we are distracted from the beautiful life that is forming right in front of us. Instead, let's believe that all those pieces: the pain, that rejection, that disappointment, that ending, has led to your life now and none of it will be wasted.

What about you? Are there things in your life about which you still feel a sense of profound disappointment? That you desperately wish could have been different, but you are powerless to change? Did you have ideals that have been crushed beyond recognition? Decisions you wish you could go back in a time machine for, and alter the course of your life?

There is nothing that will make those things go away. Life is hard, period. Life can be even crushing, at times. The exercise below is designed to help you see the good that can come out of those broken pieces. It will not make the smears on your past disappear but it will help to see something good in your life that is emerging from the terrible things that happened.

"I SOMETIMES FEEL BAD" EXERCISE

Do the following exercise if you are struggling with the fact that a second marriage is not what you had planned, and not your ideal.

1. WRITE DOWN 2-3 THINGS THAT BOTHER YOU ABOUT YOUR family situation, that are hard to accept or perhaps just don't seem fair.

Choose things that you don't have control over and cannot change. Start the statement with "I sometimes feel bad" ... or "I regret" or simply "I feel bad" Here are some examples:

- I sometimes feel bad that my first marriage didn't last and I am in a second marriage
- I feel bad that my stepchildren don't seem to like me, no matter how hard I try
- I sometimes feel bad that I couldn't have the relationship that my parents had
- I regret getting married too soon after my divorce because I didn't take time to heal

2. Now, after each statement, write down something good

that contrasts with the thing that bothers you. I will show you some examples, based on our examples from part 1:

- I sometimes feel bad that my first marriage didn't last and I had to be in a second marriage BUT I am glad that my second wife is loyal only to me.
- I feel bad that my stepchildren don't like me no matter how hard I try BUT I am grateful that they are close to their Mom and I believe they will come to trust me, in time.
- I sometimes feel bad that I couldn't have the relationship that my parents had BUT I am grateful that I learned many good relationship skills from them.
- I regret getting married too soon after my divorce because I didn't take time to heal BUT I can still take time to heal now and become whole.

6

WHY IS IT SO HARD TO LET GO?

  Remember ye not the former things, neither consider the things of old.

— ISAIAH 43:8

When you got married for the second time, did you think you were over the past? That it wouldn't affect you? Did you sweep it under the rug and vow not to think about it? Or possibly, did you get married to try to get over your past?

No matter how much we may try to deny it, it is important to remember that second marriage is *almost always* born out of a great loss. In the case of a widower, someone loses their lifetime partner from this earth. The divorced individual has gone through the loss of a marriage, which is also a devastating event.

This chapter will examine the reasons that it is so difficult to heal from our history, despite our best intentions.

HEALING IS COMPLEX

Why is it so hard to let go of the past? The short answer is that we haven't healed. But why haven't we healed? The truth is, complete healing can take a lifetime and is often complex and hard to define.

Sometimes the hurt and pain we experienced affects us in a multitude of ways that we are not even aware of. When we lose our spouse, we have lost such a huge part of who we are and what our life was about. We lose our identity as a married person and our belief that life will go on as we planned.

Even if one thinks they are completely over the pain from their past, it may resurface in a separate way and need to be dealt with.

MARRIAGE IS A CATALYST

Years before my husband and I even met, we both went through extensive counselling to help us heal from our respective divorces. We both believed we were over our past and ready to try again. The first two years of marriage, however, proved otherwise. Things from the past kept affecting us and marriage itself acted as a catalyst to bring out things that we did not realize were there.

The marriage relationship forces us to face ourselves in a way that being alone can never do. This is because being married requires a level of transparency we can never experience in any other way. Our spouse sees it all and it is this transparency which will reveal the parts of us that still need healing, the parts that still need to grow. This process will last a lifetime.

CONTINUED CONTACT WITH THE EX

Divorced individuals also have trouble letting go of the past because, if they have children, they are forced to continue seeing their former partner on a regular basis. This continual contact can make overcoming the past even more challenging.

The presence of the ex serves as a constant reminder of the hurt and anger from the past. The trouble is compounded when the ex does things that are frustrating, reminding the divorced individual of the behaviour that led to the breakup of the marriage.

Sometimes this contact continues even after the kids are grown up. Angus Jones has been divorced for over twenty-five years but the anger at his ex-wife continues to this day because of things that happen in the here-and-now. Even though the kids are now adults

OUR CHILDHOOD STILL AFFECTS US

Another reason that we may find it difficult to move on from the past is that we are still affected by events in our childhood. When we have had a troubled past before the marriage, the rejection of divorce only compounds the hurt we may have experienced as a child.

We may feel like nothing has ever worked out for us and that we are doomed to be rejected. And even after we are in a second marriage, those complex emotions can haunt us.

If your hurt goes back before the divorce or bereavement and extends into abuse, abandonment or trauma from your past, these are issues you may also need to deal with.

WE MAY BE GRIEVING

Have you considered that you might still be grieving from the loss of your spouse, whether through death or through divorce? In her book, *Sociology of the Family*, Sociologist Ron Hammond talks about how stepfamilies are often still grieving from the dissolution of the first marriage: "Stepchildren and remarried parents likely have some grief that lingers from the divorce or death of another spouse or parent."[1]

We are familiar with the grieving process when it comes to losing a spouse to death but we might not be aware that we may also grieve when we lose a spouse to divorce. If you are having trouble moving forward, it is possible that you are still stuck in your grief.

How do you know if you are still grieving? Take a look at yourself and honestly ask if you have allowed yourself to grieve for what you lost. Society is not very open and accepting of a prolonged response to a great loss, even when it comes to death. Sure, we all rally around someone for the first couple of weeks, or even the first month after a tragedy occurs but past that, the loss does not seem to be recognized. In the case of divorce, our loss is even less recognized.

I lost my mother when I was 32 years old. She was my best friend and had battled cancer for five years. A while after she had passed away, I called a friend I had not talked to for several years. She enquired about my Mom and asked me how

I was doing. I confessed to her that I was still struggling and missed her so much.

My friend then went on to tell me about one of *her* friends (who I did not know) who had recently lost someone important to her and six months later, she was doing so well and was so strong. To me, my friend's message was clear: those who don't get up and get over things are not strong and I should learn from this other woman's example.

My friend's attitude seems to be the norm. If we aren't over something within a prescribed time period, we are considered to be wallowing and need to buck up and be strong. But grief doesn't work like that. When we lose someone, we need to process the loss.

Whenever we experience a major loss, we go through distinct stages: anger, sadness and disbelief. These stages can continue to go in cycles until we come to some kind of acceptance.

If we never allow ourselves to go through that process, the grief can manifest in other ways. For example, our supressed grief may come out in anger towards our new spouse or our children. Our sadness may show itself as an inability to get close to others.

In an ideal world, we would all be able to work through our grief before getting into a new relationship but often we don't even realize we are still grieving. If you suspect you or your partner are still dealing with grief, it is important to be aware of it and then to find a way to work through it.

A trained and compassionate counsellor can be invaluable in helping work through these issues. Journaling is also an excellent way to work your way through your grief.

WE MAY BE TRAUMATIZED

Years after my divorce and before I met my current husband, I endured one of the scariest experiences of my life. I met a man I will call George. He was not especially good-looking and he definitely was not young but George had a way of talking that made you believe him and believe him I did. He had a way of making you think he could make dreams come true. In short, he was a con man.

I was pulled into a relationship with him that lasted for 1.5 years and by the end of our time together, I had been taken for everything, both financially and emotionally. It's a long story but after our relationship ended by him simply vanishing into the night, I found out that every single thing he had ever told me had been a lie.

Our whole relationship had been an illusion and the person I had known and loved had been an elaborately contrived persona. After George disappeared, I could not concentrate and constantly felt afraid and vigilant, feeling that I was in danger.

I was too embarrassed to tell people about what had happened to me but I finally found the courage to talk to a counsellor at a not-for-profit organization. This astute woman told me she suspected I was suffering from Post Traumatic Stress Disorder. (PTSD) This is a condition where after a disturbing experience, a person has recurring reactions for a period of at least one month after the event occurs.

I had never heard of this condition before but it made sense. She informed me that the best way to heal was to keep talking about my story. That was difficult because I did not want to admit to anyone that I, a well-educated intelligent woman, had been taken in by a crooked con man who had also duped dozens of women across Canada (I found out later.)

It was the most terrifying experience of my life to find out that my dream man was someone else altogether, with a completely different identity. The most frightening part was the level of deception I had been under. When we believe one thing and the world we think to be true is actually false, it can be terrifying.

For the next six months, I was almost completely useless. I did manage to work but it was extremely hard to focus. I was scared to be alone. I talked about my situation constantly to those around me. Even now, as I write about it, it feels disturbing.

Although I was never officially diagnosed by a medical doctor, I believe the counsellor was right and I had post traumatic stress disorder (PTSD) or at least a form of reaction to trauma. I had racing thoughts and felt constantly on guard and terrified. It was like being a prisoner in my own mind.

I am sharing this story, which is still hard to talk about, to help anyone who may also be suffering a traumatic reaction themselves. I am not a doctor or a psychologist, and therefore please take what I am sharing only as one layperson to another. If you suspect you may be having a stress-based response, I would implore you to look for professional help. Try to find someone who has experience working with trauma because not all therapists are trained in this area.

We experience trauma when something horrifies us or scares us and this experience leaves an imprint on our psyche that we cannot seem to shake, and we continue reacting to it over and over again by reliving it and feeling afraid.

Many of us who are in second marriages went through

something terrible to be at the point where we are marrying again. Some of us may have experienced abuse or adultery, or both. We may have been abandoned by our partner, which can be quite frightening. The first time we got married did not work as we planned: it ended, and that ending is rarely something we anticipated.

It is not surprising, therefore, that the Holmes Rahe Stress Inventory (a well-recognized way of measuring stressful events) rates the loss of a spouse to death as the most stressful events anyone can go through. Not surprising, also, is that losing a spouse to divorce is recognized as the second most stressful event a person can endure. [2]

A study published in the *Annals of Clinical Psychiatry* showed that ten percent of people who are left widowed demonstrate the symptoms of PTSD two months after their spouse passes away and that 40% of those affected had PTSD that lasted long-term.[3]

Even though every couple starts out knowing, logically, that death is going to happen to one of them eventually, I don't think we are ever truly ready for the death of someone close to us. Although the grave is inevitable, it is not "normal," no matter how common it is and it makes sense that many people experience the loss of their life partner as a type of trauma.

Divorce and the painful battle that often follows can be traumatic for those who go through it. Even before the divorce occurs, an abusive marriage may also be a source of trauma for those trapped in the nightmare of being victimized. If deception is involved, the mind games are very hard on a person psychologically.

Lisa Arends, in her book, *Lessons from the End of a Marriage*[4] writes about the horror she experienced when her husband of ten years left her a text message that ended their marriage. He then waltzed away to marry another woman he had only known for three months and left Lisa to pick up the pieces.

As the truth slowly unravelled, she found out that her husband had been living a complete double life for years. The whole situation was traumatizing for Arends and although she was never officially diagnosed with PTSD, she says her symptoms were of a similar nature. Arends explains her physical reactions to these events:

> *When my husband left, I trembled for a year. That's not just some figurative language used to convey emotion; I literally shook. For a year. My body quaked from the aftershocks of the sudden trauma, my legs constantly kicking and my hands quivering.*
>
> *Those weren't my only symptoms, either. I had flashbacks and nightmares that took me back to the to the day where I received the text that ended my marriage[5]*

Not everyone agrees that divorce or spousal abuse might cause PTSD. The Diagnostic and Statistical Manual of Mental Disorders (known as the DSM) defines PTSD[6] as being caused by "exposure to actual or threatened death, serious injury, or sexual violence"[7] This is a narrow definition and does not include common events such as divorce or bereavement, in most cases.

Whether we call it PTSD or a "trauma-based reaction," the important thing is that we know that we have experienced a frightening experience and we are reacting to it, and our actual physical symptoms cannot be denied. If the breakup was especially ugly, the chances are greater that we processed the experience as trauma.

If you suspect you may have had any kind of trauma reaction, please try to seek out an understanding counsellor who has experience dealing with trauma. It is also an excellent idea to talk to your family doctor for advice but please be aware that not all professionals recognize trauma-based reactions. This can be a long, drawn-out process, but it is necessary to get the healing that you need.

REFLECTION QUESTIONS

1. Which of the following factors apply to you:
   a. Still grieving
   b. My childhood still affects me
   c. Trauma from my past
   d. Contact with my Ex-Partner
   e. None of the above

2. WHICH OF THE FOLLOWING FACTORS DO YOU THINK MAY APPLY to your spouse:
   a. Still grieving
   b. Childhood still affects them
   c. Trauma from the past
   d. Contact with the ex-partner
   e. None of the above

7

YOU MIGHT NEED HEALING IF...

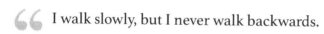 I walk slowly, but I never walk backwards.

— ABRAHAM LINCOLN

*H*ow can you tell if you still need healing from the past? This chapter has a list of clues you can look for, to see if you might need some more emotional healing.

YOU LACK TRUST

One of the most common signs of not being over the past is distrust. Before marrying Elise, Alex Roca was married to a woman who cheated on him more than once and then moved his children to another state.

Elise explains, "For my husband, it was a trust issue. He always thought I was a cheat. He always had a fear that I was going to leave."

When you see your mate *through* your past, you may assume that your spouse is doing something that he isn't doing. Your spouse may even say to you, "But I am not "Rob." I am me. I would never do that!"

Misinterpreting your spouse's motives comes from a lack of trust in the current relationship. My husband had real difficulty trusting me after his divorce and I have often looked him in the eye and said, "I am on your side." We need to stop the expectations that our current spouse is going to do (or is currently doing) something that our ex did.

YOU ARE JEALOUS

When my husband and I first got married, I constantly brought up the name of his ex-girlfriend he had dated after his divorce. I did this before we got married, and then continued afterwards. In one of my many turbulent moments, I yelled at him, "Go back to her!"

The funny part (now) is that he never once mentioned her name. It was me who saw her in my mind, haunted by this woman that I was sure was prettier than me, funnier than me and probably still secretly in love with him, just waiting for our marriage to break up and free him to go back to her.

I thought I was over my past, but I obviously was not. My insecurity turned me into this emotional, jealous woman who was constantly convinced my husband was looking at other women, thinking about his ex-girlfriend and possibly cheating on me. Maybe all at the same time!

What caused this absurdity? Needless to say, I was extremely insecure. My last relationship had been with a con man who had lied about every single thing in his life. In my twenties, I had been extremely trusting and naïve but the experience of being deceived had left me constantly suspicious.

When I saw certain behaviour in my husband that was similar to what I had seen before, I assumed he was the same kind of man that I had been with before and I reacted that way. In reality, he was very different but my fears did not allow me to see that.

If you are jealous and insecure about your relationship, this is a very good sign that you may not be over your past. Unless your spouse has given good reason to doubt her, consider that you are probably reacting out of fear from past rejection and betrayal.

YOU ARE BITTER

Feeling bitter can be another sign that your past is still strongly influencing your present. Bitterness can sneak up on us when we are not looking and make us into a different person. We may start to feel resentful of someone for no apparent reason or snap at a friend when they have done nothing to deserve it. These are all signs that we may be bitter without even realizing it.

Bitterness can make us feel cynical with an edge of anger towards those around us, unable to get too close or hope for something good. If you feel a sense of quiet anger that seethes out without you wanting it to, there is a good chance you are still bitter from what has happened to you in the past.

YOU FEEL DEFEATED

As humans, we love success and that motivates us to keep going. Failure, on the other hand, demotivates us. When we experience a devastating failure, our immediate instinct is to run away and never try again. The loss of a marriage can feel like a failure and when it looks like this marriage won't work, either, we may feel defeated.

When my husband and I used to argue, he would say to me, "Well, there you go. I suck as a husband." He felt that he had failed at his first marriage and whenever I brought up an issue, he felt that he was failing again. The fear of failure was strong in him and made it hard for him to hear my concerns.

If we feel defeated, it is hard to make the effort to work things out and try in our relationship. Instead, we retreat and avoid issues, convinced that there is no point in trying. If you feel defeated whenever you experience difficulties in your marriage, it may be because you still feel sadness over your past relationship not working out.

YOU REPEAT YOUR MISTAKES

One of the most important ways that we can tell we haven't processed what went wrong in our first relationship is that we eventually start to repeat the mistakes of our first marriage.

Why do we do this? We do this because we are putting all the blame on our former spouse for the marriage breaking down and are not owning up to what we contributed.

Whenever a relationship breaks up, there are always two people that contributed to problems and there are always lessons to be learned. If we do not take the time to learn from the first relationship, we will simply bring our mistakes and weaknesses into the second marriage. Things that we did to trigger our first spouse will often have the same affect on our current spouse and this is when we see history repeating itself.

For the first years of our marriage, neither my husband nor I had let go of our past and we took it out on each other in horrible ways. Through prayer, counselling and hard work, we gradually let go of the past and started looking towards the future. I truly understand how difficult this is to do but it may be the thing that saves your marriage.

REFLECTION QUESTIONS

1. On a scale of 1-10, how much do you think you have let go of the past?

2. USING THE SAME SCALE, HOW MUCH DO YOU THINK YOUR spouse has let go of the past?

3. WHICH OF THE FOLLOWING SIGNS DO YOU EXHIBIT IN your life?
   a. You lack trust
   b. You are jealous
   c. You are bitter
   d. You feel defeated
   e. You are repeating your mistakes
   f. None of the above

. . .

4. WHICH OF THE FOLLOWING SIGNS DOES YOUR SPOUSE EXHIBIT in their life?

    a. They lack trust

    b. They are jealous

    c. They are bitter

    d. They feel defeated

    e. They are repeating their mistakes

    f. None of the above

8

TAKE OWNERSHIP

God has entrusted me with myself.

— EPICTETUS

hen Elise Roca and her husband Alex got married over ten years ago, it was a second marriage for each of them but they had distinctive ways of dealing with the past.

After her divorce, Elise remained single for many years, living alone and focusing on taking care of her children. She says that her past really wasn't an issue by the time she finally decided to get married again. Her faith had helped her get over things and move on. Elise explains, "To *me*, that's not who I was anymore. I was a new person."

Alex, on the other hand, had just recently become divorced and was still hurting and raw when he decided to marry again. For the first few years they were together, Alex was constantly nervous about whether his new wife would cheat on him and walk away. Elise's continual reassurance and patience helped him to finally believe that this time would be different. She says, "I kept telling him, 'I won't leave. I won't walk away.'"

Letting go is harder for some of us than others and telling someone to let go of the past is much easier than doing it. So, if you are still focused on the past and unable to let go, let's look at some strategies for facilitating healing.

Please be aware that this process can take years and go in stages. I have distilled the process down to a few neat chapters in this book but that does not mean it is a tidy, quick process. The important thing is that you are growing and making some kind of progress. Don't expect that it will always be a swift turnaround.

It is also very important to note that these principles apply for whatever part of the past is still affecting you, including your previous marriage, other past romantic relationships or things that happened to you as a child or teenager. The lessons in the following two chapters can also be applied to things within your *present* marriage that you are having a troublesome time letting go of.

FOUR STEPS TO HEALING FROM THE PAST

The next section will outline four steps for moving on. If you are a widow or widower who is struggling with moving forward, these steps also apply to you, with the exception of step 2 (take responsibility.) Here are the steps:

1. Acknowledge your feelings
2. Take responsibility
3. Forgive yourself and others

4. Change your thinking

AGAIN, PLEASE REMEMBER THAT THESE FOUR STEPS MAY APPEAR easy when they are distilled down to a simple list but they can take years of work and uncovering the onion layers. This is not a quick fix. But these four steps give a framework for healing from the past, which may include a past marriage, hurts in your current relationship, childhood trauma or an old boyfriend or girlfriend.

For the rest of this chapter, we will look at steps one and two: admitting how you feel and taking responsibility. In Chapter 10, we will examine the importance of forgiveness and changing your thinking.

ACKNOWLEDGE YOUR FEELINGS

The first step for healing from the past is to acknowledge that you *haven't* healed from the past. It is ironic but unless we acknowledge a problem, we have no hope of fixing it. When we are completely blind to the patterns that are working themselves in our life, they continue to go unchecked. It is when we are able to see the patterns and acknowledge them that we start on the path to healing.

Often, we don't realize we are still harbouring some old emotions until it starts to show up in our relationship. For example, we snap at our spouse for no apparent reason and we realize that we still have anger to deal with.

In the last chapter, we examined the signs of having not let go. If you see these signs in yourself, it is time to do some self-examination. A counsellor or even a good listening friend can helpful in getting to the root of things. Prayer can be a powerful way of getting in touch with your deeper motives.

Part of the problem is that we are so conditioned to want to be strong that we may feel ashamed to say we aren't over something. Don't let embarrassment stop you from being vulnerable and moving towards healing. Anyone who has gone through a great loss like you have, struggles to put the pieces back together and not let the past rule their life. It is a process that can take years.

At the time of your loss (bereavement or divorce) you may not have had the time or space to recognize the sadness that you felt over what had happened. When a crisis hits, one usually goes into survival mode. You have to figure out what to do and how to get through it financially and practically. If you have children, you have meet their needs. Processing the emotions is often a low priority.

You may also be nervous about admitting the past is still an issue because it may feel like a threat to your current partner. If we admit we are still bothered by something an ex did, it may seem like that ex is playing too big a role in our life. For this reason, I encourage you to involve your spouse in your journey, if he is open to being involved. It can be a bit scary to seem like you are "going backwards" by reliving some of these memories but remember that your goal is to let go, so that you can be truly there for your partner *now*.

Remember, though, that losing a spouse, whether through marriage or death, is a multi-layered loss. If you haven't done so, take some time to really reflect on what you lost when you lost your spouse. Some examples are that you lost your identity as a married person, you were deprived of someone who knew you better than anyone on earth and you lost a family. You suffered the loss of your dreams.

To help you get in touch with your emotions, you may wish to journal. Use a journal to document the emotions that you are going through. Allow yourself the liberty to write freely. You might go for walks alone and just spend time thinking, or praying. If you are a believer, talk to the Lord about it. A good therapist can also help to draw these emotions out.

Whatever the feelings are: sadness, anger, disappointment, confusion: acknowledge them so that you can move past them, thus taking away their power from your life.

TAKE RESPONSIBILITY

The next step in letting go of the past is to take responsibility for *your* part in what happened. This can be hard to do, especially if we believe that we were the victims. In every breakup, however, there are always two sides to the story and two people contributing to the problems.

The purpose of this step is not to make you feel guilty or to condemn yourself but it is for you to take responsibility for your part in what happened in your past.

If you want to do well in your second marriage, it is very important to examine what happened in the first marriage, so that you do not keep repeating the same old patterns. The next exercise is designed to help you take an honest look at your previous relationship(s) and see how both of you contributed to things not working.

As a disclaimer, I want to say that if you were abused or cheated on, that wasn't your fault. But there were probably things that led to choosing someone that would be abusive or disloyal. You were not responsible for the other person's actions but you did choose to be with that person. What was it *in you* that *led you* to choose this particular person?

I know this from my personal experience. Throughout much of my adult life, I made poor choices in romance. No matter what I did, I always seem to end up hurt and alone.

I chose one man who was completely deceptive. I chose another man who physically threatened me by punching walls. I dated men who had no concept of loyalty and used me until they threw me out.

It was not until I saw the common thread throughout these relationships that things started to change. The common thread was me. Yes, I had been with cheaters, users and abusers. But I picked them.

This exercise is about seeing how you contributed to the life that you have had, even if it was because you chose someone who cheated on you or abused you. When we can start to see how we have made the choices that shaped our lives, we start to have more control.

"DIGGING UP BONES" EXERCISE

This exercise is designed to see how patterns from your first marriage (or other relationships) may be continuing in your current marriage. Write down the answers to the following questions.

I. WHAT WAS THE MAIN ISSUE THAT YOU AND YOUR EX FOUGHT about? Be as specific as possible.

. . .

EXAMPLE: FIGHTING OVER WHO DOES THE HOUSEWORK.

2. FOR THIS ISSUE, WHAT DID YOUR EX-PARTNER DO THAT contributed to the problem?

EXAMPLE: HE ALWAYS COMPLAINED THAT THE HOUSE WASN'T clean enough but he never helped.

3. WHAT DID YOU TO CONTRIBUTE TO THE PROBLEM?

EXAMPLE: I ALWAYS NAGGED HIM AND GOT REALLY ANGRY AT HIM.

4. IS THIS ISSUE A CONCERN IN YOUR CURRENT MARRIAGE? If yes, answer the following questions.

5. HOW IS YOUR SPOUSE CONTRIBUTING TO THE ISSUE?

EXAMPLE: *HE NEVER CLEANS UP AFTER HIMSELF.*

6. WHAT ARE YOU DOING TO CONTRIBUTE TO THE PROBLEM?

. . .

EXAMPLE: I ALWAYS NAG AND YELL AT HIM

7. ARE YOU HANDLING THIS ISSUE IN THE SAME WAY OR IN A different way than you handled it before? How so?

EXAMPLE: I HANDLE IT THE SAME WAY I DID BEFORE. I YELL AND get angry.

8. HOW COULD YOU HANDLE THIS ISSUE IN A DIFFERENT WAY, TO get different results?

9

FORGIVENESS

66 Forgive us our debts, as we forgive our debtors.

— MATTHEW 6:12

*T*he third step required for healing from our past is forgiveness. For many years, I struggled with forgiveness because I thought it meant letting people off the hook. When I began to realize that forgiveness did not mean I was justifying what they had done, it became easier.

Forgiveness means that we are no longer responsible for judging or punishing someone else for what they have done wrong against us. It means letting go and letting God deal with their consequences.

WHY FORGIVENESS IS SO DIFFICULT

It is not always an easy thing to do, however. In fact, forgiveness can feel like it's ripping our soul apart. It is hard to let it go because it seems so unfair. It is unfair that we were blindsided by a divorce. Unfair that we were betrayed or abused or neglected.

We want to hold on to it, in order to protect ourselves and the part of us that knows how wrong it was. We fear that if we forgive, we may be saying that the hurt parts of ourselves didn't really matter. It can actually feel like we are abandoning ourselves.

THEY KNOW NOT WHAT THEY DO

One of the most famous quotes about forgiveness comes from the story of Jesus on the cross. While he was hanging, bleeding and broken, he cried out these puzzling words. "Father, forgive them, for they know not what they do." He asked his Father to forgive the men who plotted his death.

The Scriptures say that men in positions of power plotted and schemed to have Jesus crucified by the Roman governor. I have sometimes wondered about these words, "they know not what they do."

Although these men seemed to know exactly what they were doing, they were likely not aware of the long-term consequences of what was happening. They could only see their own petty power struggles and their own desires. They were blind to the pain of anyone else.

What if we could adopt these same words for ourselves? "Forgive our ex, because they did not know what they were doing." And let's face it: they probably didn't know what they were doing – not fully. In some cases, it may have been pure weakness on their part.

In other scenarios, perhaps the person did not have the emotional capacity to understand anyone's feelings but their own. For others, they were caught in a passion or habit that would destroy many a life, including theirs. When we forgive them, we are not saying that what they did was okay but we are saying that they really did not understand the extent of the consequences.

The ones that wronged us had a blind spot in them that blocked them from seeing how much hurt they really caused. Whether it was mental illness, a bad childhood, simple selfishness or even psychopathy, their eyes were blinded to the consequences of what they were doing. They really did not know what they did, often until it was too late.

BITTERNESS IS A POISON

When we got married, my husband and I both had bitterness against people in our past and the result on our marriage was devastating. Unforgiveness made us closed to love and quick to judge. Our new marriage was being poisoned by the actions done against us in the past.

Our bitterness was understandable. We both felt wronged. We had both tried to be good partners but had been rejected. The truth is, though, no matter how justified the bitterness, it is still a poison that will destroy an individual and a marriage.

FORGIVENESS SETS YOU FREE

Forgiveness was not an easy path for us. It was not automatic but when we were able to forgive, it was like our very souls had been set free. When bitterness no longer gripped us with its heavy talons, we were free to trust the other person and to see them as they really were. We stopped seeing each other through the filter of the past and saw the loving person in front of us.

When you can't forgive, it turns into bitterness and hurts you more than it hurts anyone else. Forgiveness frees you to begin each day afresh. Forgiveness is not always a quick and automatic process. We may believe that we have forgiven someone but then a trigger happens, and we realize that we are still carrying around resentment. That is okay -- like an onion, the process happens in layers.

It is also important to note that forgiveness does not mean that you have to let the person who hurt you back into your close personal circle. We can forgive someone but we can keep up our boundaries toward them.

WHO DO YOU NEED TO FORGIVE?

First, you need to forgive yourself for the mistakes you made in your first marriage and in any other relationships you were in. Maybe you see how you could have done things differently and kept your marriage together. Perhaps you feel you should not have even married in the first place. Whatever it is that you are blaming yourself for, forgive yourself first.

Next, forgive the people in your past relationships. This includes your ex-wife or husband if you were the one that was married before. It also includes past girlfriends, boyfriends, or even people that you may have had a brief encounter with, that didn't work out. You may also discover that you need to forgive a parent or someone else from your childhood.

The last one sounds a bit strange but bear with me. If your souse was married before, forgive your partner's ex-spouse. When you get married, you learn a lot about your spouse's ex and see how your husband or wife was affected by their actions. It is easy to start to develop feelings of hate or anger towards this person who may have caused your partner pain, especially if he is still taking it out on you.

LOOK AT YOUR THOUGHTS

The final step in healing from your past is to have a look at your thoughts. It is very difficult to change your feelings but it is very possible to change your thoughts, and transformed thoughts lead to transformed feelings.

Dr. Caroline Leaf, a renowned neurobiologist originally from South Africa, in her book, *Switch Your Brain: The Key to Peak Happiness, Thinking, and Health* describes how controlling our thoughts leads to better functioning in every area of our life:

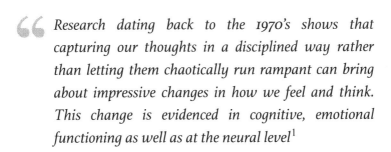

Research dating back to the 1970's shows that capturing our thoughts in a disciplined way rather than letting them chaotically run rampant can bring about impressive changes in how we feel and think. This change is evidenced in cognitive, emotional functioning as well as at the neural level[1]

What she is saying is that when we are aware of our thoughts and then stop the thoughts that we don't want, we are able to both think *and* feel better. When we go into a second marriage, we are sometimes carrying around mental baggage that we don't even realize is there.

These thoughts could have originated from the second marriage or may even go back to childhood. We pick up negative thoughts from being bullied, from our own self-doubt and from negative experiences. Wherever these thoughts come from, we have more power than we realize to start to change them. Remember that this is not a one-time thing. You may need to go through these steps several times, for different issues, as they come to mind.

Let's look at an example from one of our interview couples. You may recall Alex, whose first wife cheated on him. His thoughts were telling him that all women cheat and this made him super-suspicious of Elise. The thought (that women cheat on their men) was affecting him and carried with it a very negative emotion (fear). This fear was affecting his current marriage.

When Alex was able to look clearly at his wife and see that her loyalty was what he loved about her, he was able to change his thoughts, and his feelings followed.

A specific way that you can change your thinking, when you mistrust your spouse because of your past, is to remember what drew you to your current spouse in the first place. Then, when you react to something your spouse does, ask yourself if you are reacting to your real spouse, or just reacting to the memory of your past.

Then look at your reasons for loving him. Remind yourself of why you married this person and remind yourself of these qualities. Also, remind yourself of your commitment to work it out with them, no matter how difficult. This next exercise will help you to do this.

"WHAT I LIKE ABOUT YOU" EXERCISE

This exercise asks you to write down a list of eight (or more if you like!) things that you like about your spouse.

You can be as specific or as general as you like. A specific example might be "I like how Judy smiles at me in the mornings." A general example might be "I like how Brent is hard-working."

If your spouse is open to it, try this exercise together. If not, that's okay because you will still benefit from it because it is designed to help change *your* thinking about what happens in your marriage.

1. FILL IN THE FOLLOWING SENTENCE EIGHT TIMES:

I LIKE HOW ...

IF YOU START TO JUDGE YOUR SPOUSE THROUGH THE FILTER OF your past, remind yourself of the things that like about your spouse. *This* is who he or she is, not the person from your past.

WHEN YOU FEEL INSECURE

66 Life is like riding a bicycle. To keep your balance,
you must keep moving.

— ALBERT EINSTEIN

One of the funniest skits that Carole Burnett ever did
dealt with the issue of insecurity in a marriage. The
sketch is called Wrong Number[1] and features a husband and
his wife asleep on their matching twin beds in the middle of
the night, when the telephone rings.

The man answers it, says "hello," and then hangs up. After
he does, the woman asks who it was. He says it he doesn't
know because the person didn't say anything and just hung
up. For most of us, that would be enough of an explanation.
Wrong numbers are not that unusual, but for this insecure
woman, that is just the beginning!

She keeps interrogating him, working herself up in a tizzy,

convinced that the wrong number must have been an elaborate scheme for her husband to communicate with his lover. Finally, he manages to satisfy her and get her to go back to sleep.

This skit received a lot of laughs because we see how ridiculous insecurity can be, and many of us can relate! Like many of Burnett's sketches, however, there is one more catch that makes it even funnier. After the husband has managed to calm his hysterical wife down and she has gone back to sleep, he takes his bed covers off and reveals that he is fully dressed. He then tries to sneak out of the room, presumably to meet his mistress.

This is our worst fear when we suffer from insecurity: that our wild fears really *are* true and that if we let go of the jealousy, even just for a moment, we will miss something and our spouse will sneak out and do the thing that we fear so much, like the husband does in this skit.

Do you ever feel insecure or jealous? If so, this chapter is for you. I understand, because jealousy used to be a huge issue for me, too, as I shared in chapter eight. I know how challenging it is to get over the fears that your partner might cheat and to stress endlessly about whether or not your spouse can be trusted.

Overcoming insecurity is one of the most difficult things we must do, especially if we have been cheated on, lied to, abused or abandoned. It takes everything in us to learn to trust again.

My insecurity came partially because I had been the victim of infidelity before. The fear also stemmed from the bullying I experienced as a child. Part of me felt like I was never quite good enough for anyone. I tried not to let anyone know how insecure I was but all that insecurity was unleashed in my marriage.

My jealousy and insecurity did a lot of damage. The lowest point was when I screamed at my husband to go back to his ex-girlfriend because I was convinced that he probably loved her more than he loved me, even though he had not expressed anything like that, *ever*, since we had been together.

It also led to snooping around in his things and finding some old notes his ex-girlfriend had written him when they were together. He did not even know that the letters were there but I found them, and it was like he had a full-blown affair on me.

It is embarrassing to admit how insecure I was but I hope that by me sharing this weakness, it may help anyone that struggles with insecurity and jealousy to know it is possible to overcome it. Thinking back to how I felt and acted then, it feels ridiculous. Like Carol in the "Wrong Number" sketch, jealousy and insecurity can get a hold of our mind and make us irrational and out-of-control.

First a disclaimer. In a few cases, jealousy is legitimate. If our spouse is a huge flirt or into pornography, we have reason to feel like he is giving someone else the attention that should be reserved for us.

Sometimes there is actual sexual adultery going on and that nagging feeling we have is the confirmation that the marriage is broken and someone else has gotten in between us. If jealousy is from a real cause, we don't have an insecurity problem, we have a loyalty problem and that is a different issue.

But if there is no real reason to be jealous except that you have learned from your past that it seems that most women or most men cheat, then you need to get this feeling in check.

First, you may need to go through the steps for letting go of the past as outlined in the last two chapters. Then, you need to make a choice to trust your spouse. You might be scared to do that because what if they cheat, like every other person you have been with?

Well, it's true that it is possible that it could happen again. Anything can happen but the more you trust your spouse and build the love between you, the less likely this will happen. This was what I finally had to do to stop the insecurity: I had to make a decision to trust my husband.

Then, if you have an insecure thought, you can talk about it with your spouse and ask, "Is this true?" and they can simply say "No, it's not true." And then you can say, "Okay, sorry, that's just my *insecure self* coming up again. I believe you."

REFLECTION QUESTIONS

1. On a scale of 1-10, how insecure are you in your marriage?

1 2 3 4 5 6 7 8 9 10

ANSWER THE FOLLOWING QUESTIONS IF YOU SCORED YOURSELF AS five or higher.

A. HAS YOUR SPOUSE EVER GIVEN YOU A REASON TO BE INSECURE, with his or her behaviour?

· · ·

B. Do you think the insecurity is stemming from something in your past?

C. Can you make a decision to trust your spouse?

2. On a scale of 1-10, how insecure do you think your spouse is?

1 2 3 4 5 6 7 8 9 10

If you scored him or her as five or above, answer the following questions.

a. Has you ever given your spouse a reason to be insecure, with your behaviour?

B. If you have given them reason to be insecure, have you made an effort to stop that behaviour and seek their forgiveness?

C. Do you think the insecurity is stemming from something in his or her past?

D. Can you ask your spouse to make a decision to trust you?

LEARNING TO ACCEPT YOUR STORY

 And now you know -- the rest of the story.

— PAUL HARVEY

One of my most painful childhood memories was when I was ten or eleven years old. Our family attended a Baptist church which had a large balcony overlooking the sanctuary. I was walking down the aisle, when a big spitball flew through the air from the balcony and landed right on my head.

Looking up, I saw a boy named Donnie looking down on me, laughing with his friend. I was humiliated and felt so dirty from this act of bullying. It felt like I was the ultimate piece of trash, to be spat upon.

As a child, I went through severe bullying by my classmates. I was the kid that other kids would tease mercilessly. Because I did not fight back, the teasing seemed endless.

For most of my adult life, I have not talked much about the bullying I endured, except to counsellors. This year, I was asked to speak at a ladies' meeting at our church. I decided to share my story of the spitball episode with the ladies.

I then went on to talk about how we need to show love to one another in the church. Sharing this story was very hard to do because I was worried about what people would think. I persevered, though, and told my story, along with the teaching on how important it is to care for others.

And you know what? Once the words had come out of my mouth, the hurt from the incident seemed to lose any power it still had over me, even after all these years. I felt free, as a result of sharing it with others. When other people came up and told me how much it had touched them, they didn't know that it had healed me, too.

Sharing your story can be a tremendous healing tool, if you are ready for it. I would only recommend doing so if you are far along in your healing process. If you are still raw and hurting all the time, save this exercise for when you are ready.

This tool is about learning to accept your story. It may not be what you wanted it to be and it's not what you dreamed about but it is *your* story. It is beautiful in its own way.

In our lifetime, we have all been exposed to thousands of stories. We read stories in books, we see them on television shows and we watch them in movies. We also know, personally, the stories of many of the people we grew up with, work with, and have as friends.

Everyone has a different story. A story is not wrong or

right. It just is. People in the story may have done something wrong but the story itself is not wrong.

This exercise challenges you to share your story in a non-emotional manner. Then, whenever you are tempted to compare your story now to your previous story, remind yourself that that was a previous chapter.

Now you are working on a new chapter. There is nothing you can do about your past. It is part of your story and you are continuing to write your story today. Remember that if you would like to have a printable version of all the exercises and questions in this book, you will soon be able to purchase the accompanying workbook, *Second Marriage: An Insider's Guide to Hope, Healing & Love Workbook*, on Amazon, or as a free download at http://secondmarriage.xyz/sign-free-resources-page.

"TELL YOUR STORY" EXERCISE

This exercise is designed to tell your story, either to another person or by writing it down. I will list a series of questions to answer.

POINTERS

• Remember to include both the good and the bad. If you focus only on the negative, you may slow down your healing by seeing your past as all bad. If you focus only on the positive, you may slow down your healing by idealizing the past instead of looking at it realistically.

• If you choose to tell the story in person, make sure you choose someone who can be an objective listener. Do not choose someone who will react too emotionally to hearing your story.

• The goal of this exercise is to tell the story in a straightforward, factual manner, so try to not focus on your emotions too much but rather on the facts of what happened.

• Make sure that you choose a time when your children are not close by, although you may wish to share the story with them when they are older.

• If you are in therapy, this might be a good thing to do with your therapist, if he is willing.

• If you choose to write your story out, take as much as time as you need, coming back as many as times as you need to, to finish writing your story out.

The Questions

Answer the following questions regarding your first marriage.

1. HOW DID THE TWO OF YOU MEET?

2. HOW LONG DID YOU DATE?

3. HOW OLD WERE YOU WHEN YOU GOT MARRIED?

4. WHAT CHILDREN DID YOU HAVE, IF ANY?

. . .

5. WHAT PLACES DID YOU LIVE DURING YOUR MARRIAGE?

6. WHAT DID THE TWO OF YOU ENJOY DOING TOGETHER?

7. DID THE TWO YOU ARGUE OR FIGHT A LOT? WHAT WERE THE arguments or fights about?

Answer these questions if your marriage ended in divorce.

8. WHAT PRECIPITATED THE BREAKUP?

9. WAS THERE ADULTERY, ABUSE OR ABANDONMENT INVOLVED? Which one(s)?

10. HOW DID YOU COPE WITH THE DIVORCE?

Answer these questions if your first spouse passed away. (Please omit if any of these questions are too painful or triggering. Do these only if you feel ready.)

11. DID YOU KNOW THAT YOUR SPOUSE WAS GOING TO PASS beforehand or was it a surprise?

12. IF YOU KNEW, WHAT WAS THE TIME BEFORE HER/HIS PASSING like?

. . .

13. WERE YOU THERE AT HER/HIS DEATH? IF IT IS NOT TOO painful, how was this time?

14. HOW DO YOU HONOUR THEM IN YOUR LIFE NOW?

Answer the following questions regarding your time between marriages.

15. DID YOU DATE ANYONE ELSE IN BETWEEN YOUR TWO marriages? If so, who did you date?

16. DID YOU HAVE ANY *SERIOUS* RELATIONSHIPS IN BETWEEN marriages? Who were they? What were the main reasons that this/these relationship(s) did not work out?

ONCE YOU HAVE SHARED THIS PART OF YOUR STORY, I WANT YOU to imagine a little cabinet in your mind. In the cabinet, there are several drawers. One of the drawers is empty. Open it, and place that story in the drawer. It is part of your history but now you are placing it in its right place.

You are now working on an exciting new chapter, your second marriage. The next few questions are about the early history of your second marriage.

Answer the following questions regarding your current marriage.

. . .

17. How did the two of you meet?

18. How long did you date?

19. Did you ever break up? What caused the break up?

20. Where did you get married? What was your wedding like?

IV

HEALING YOUR MARRIAGE

This next section is the fun part! We will look at how people *can* stay in love for the long haul, and some amazing tips for keeping, or rekindling the romance between you.

We will also look at how it is just as important to be good friends, as it is to be good lovers. And then we take a brief look at handling conflict better in your marriage. Finally, we will look at how opposites can make the best couples!

1 2

ARE WE DESTINED FOR LOVE?

 ...for love is strong as death.

— SONG OF SOLOMON 8:6B

*A*re you a fan of chick flick movies? If so, you may recognize this common trope from many romantic comedies. It goes like this. Girl is dating Boring Guy. He doesn't understand her, but she doesn't know what she is missing until she meets Exciting Guy. She feels drawn to Exciting Guy but can't be with him because she is still committed to Boring Guy.

They go through a long series of obstacles until the girl is finally won over by Exciting Guy. She dumps Boring Guy and we all cheer. Hooray! The two of them are in love and have that elusive connection that she never would have had with Boring Guy. It's almost like magic. And let's be honest, many of the women go home wishing their love life could be a little more magical, like the movie.

We call this connection, the feeling of "being one" romantic love, eros, or passion. Without it, most of us would never get married or have children. This is the kind of love that is supposed to make the world go around! We all look for this kind of love when we get married. No one wants to feel like they are just married to their roommate.

But what if you don't feel this kind of love for your spouse now? What if the passion is gone and you're not sure if it was ever there? Does that mean that the marriage is dead? That you are doomed to a stale relationship?

Most of us have experienced that lack of passion in our marriage at one time or another. This is why many people give up and conclude that romance is only for the young. When we are in a second marriage, it is even harder to maintain that ardent desire because we are often dealing with so much stress.

In this chapter, we are going to look at two studies done by scientists at Stony Brook University, in New York, that will help us better understand how couples can develop and maintain a sense of passion. In the two chapters that follow, we will examine how we can develop that sense of delight and love in our own marriages.

ROMANCE CAN LAST A LIFETIME

The first study, called "Neural Correlates of Long-Term Intense Romantic Love," from Stony Brook University looked at the *brain activity* of a group of couples who reported themselves as still being in love after many years.

What they found was that these older couples had very similar chemical reactions in their brain to young couples who were freshly in love.[1] It was almost as if their brains thought they *were* young and in love: it was the same chemical reaction.

The study showed that the majority of these older in-love couples, who had been married an average of 25 years, had the following characteristics:

1. They made love frequently.
2. They had a strong emotional attachment to each other.
3. They were good friends.

Remember, these couples had been married for an average of twenty-five years but their feelings were still strong! When the scientists tried to find some common characteristics that the in-love couples shared, these three common threads stood out.

The couples had a strong focus on sex in their marriage. They did not give up on physical love but continued to find ways to please each other in bed. Secondly, they were emotionally close: they were warm with each other. Lastly, their friendship was strong.

This study contradicts the commonly held belief that romantic love always fades away after the first year or two of marriage. It also shows that the feelings of being "in love" are not magical, as the movies suggest. Instead, these "in-love" feelings corresponded with three distinct factors: emotional intimacy, strong friendship and physical closeness.

QUESTIONS THAT LEAD TO EMOTIONAL INTIMACY

From the last study, we found that emotional intimacy was one of the factors for couples experiencing a feeling of being in love. The next study, also from Stony Brook University, demonstrates that feeling close to someone comes from sharing deep, personal things about one's self. In other words, you can build emotional intimacy by sharing intimacies with another human being.

In this very encouraging study, called "The Experimental Generation of Interpersonal Closeness,"[2] led by researcher Dr. Arthur Aron, students in a beginner's psychology class were paired up with another student that they did not know personally. The pair of students then proceeded to ask (and answer) a set of increasingly personal questions.

After a total of 36 questions, the students were then asked how close they felt to the person they had been paired up with. What the researchers found was that the two people felt quite close after asking and answering these questions of one another, in spite of the fact that they had been complete strangers just an hour before.

A surprising thing about the study was that even people who scored as complete opposites in key areas, still felt this sense of closeness with one another, which shows that it is the *sharing of one's self* that creates closeness, not necessarily agreeing on everything. In chapter 16, we will look more at how couples who are opposite can get along and even capitalize on their differences.

This study suggests that the key ingredient to feeling close to another human being is sharing deep personal communication with them. It also demonstrates that we can feel a sense of intimacy with someone, even if they are quite different from us.

What we can learn from this, for our marriage, is how important it is to share our heart honestly with our spouse. When two people try to hide their true feelings from one another, in order to keep the peace, they are missing out on the one thing that could actually build the feeling of closeness, in spite of the problems.

I have found this very thing to be true in my own marriage. I have a tendency to keep things to myself until they pile up. I avoid talking to my husband because I know he is busy and I don't want to bother him. I find, though, that keeping things from him leads to distance between us. As soon as I share, however, that feeling of intimacy returns.

THIS STUDY IN POPULAR MEDIA

A few years ago, this particular study was highlighted in the mainstream media when The New York Times published an article called *To Fall in Love with Anyone, Do This*[3].

In this article, writer Mandy Len Catron decided to test these questions out on a male acquaintance, to see if asking the same questions that Dr. Aron used in the study would make her and her male friend feel closer.

Catron said she had heard somewhere that staring into someone's eyes for four minutes would also aid in falling in love, so they tried that, too. According to the author, the two of them *did* fall in love, after a few weeks, but she does not credit the questions exclusively for them getting together.

When I first read this article two years ago, I decided to try part of the experiment on my husband. He looked up from his laptop to see me staring directly into his eyes. Unfortunately, the results were not exactly what I was hoping for: he actually got angry with me because he thought I was mocking him.

The New York Times article gained a great deal of media attention. One website, called *Soul Pancake*, decided to do their own little experiment. They found six couples, at various stages of relationship (from complete strangers to married for many years) and asked them to stare into each other's eyes for four minutes straight.

The video[4] shows their reactions as they progress through the four minutes of staring into one another's eyes. All of them seem to experience a profound sense of intimacy, which is very moving to watch.

In this chapter, we have examined two studies, plus one quasi-experiment about staring into someone's eyes. The conclusions from these studies were the following:

a. Being friends is part of staying in love

b. Sex is important for staying in love

c. Emotional closeness keeps you in love

d. Intimate conversations lead to a feeling of closeness

e. We can be opposites but still feel close

REFLECTION QUESTIONS

1. Have you ever longed for more passion in your marriage?

2. HAVE YOU EVER KNOWN AN OLDER MARRIED COUPLE WHO ARE still very passionate about one another?

. . .

3. WHICH (IF ANY) OF THE FOLLOWING FINDINGS FROM THE studies/video did you find surprising?

    a. Intimate conversations lead to a feeling of closeness

    b. Eye contact can be powerful

    c. We can be opposites but still feel close

    d. Being friends is part of staying in love

    e. Sex is important for staying in love

    f. None of these were surprising to me

13

TO KNOW YOU IS TO LOVE YOU

66 *Keep love in your heart. A life without it is like a sunless garden when the flowers are dead.*

— OSCAR WILDE

The *Newlywed Game*[1] was a TV game show from the seventies that invited newlywed couples to answer questions about their new spouse. The couple that got the most correct answers won a large-ticket item such a fridge or a trip, and those who did poorly, well, it looked like their marriages might be in trouble!

We all long to be known, especially by the person we have sworn our lives to. In fact, the word for "make love," in the Bible is the word "know." [2] In Hebrew, the original language of the Old Testament, the word for taking part in sexual activity was the same word used for "comprehend" or "become aware."

This implies that making love was considered an integral

part of two people knowing each other in the deepest way possible. We long to be known but often the complication of second marriage can make it more difficult to achieve this closeness. Instead, we sometimes become more focused on winning the argument and defending ourselves.

Even if our conflicts are not loud and in the open, we can be quietly hostile to each other, shutting the other person out with distractions, such as work or the Internet.

This was the case for Betty and Angus Jones. They did not fight loudly but there was a sense of quiet hostility in their home. Betty felt a great deal of frustration when it seemed that her husband was avoiding conflict. Angus admits, "I was a conflict avoider. Sometimes, I wouldn't talk to her for four days."

How do we break through and really get to know each other? Here are four suggestions for helping us truly "know" each other as husband and wife:

1. Take time to talk
2. Look at each other
3. Grab a few minutes
4. Make some sweet, sweet love

TAKE TIME TO TALK

When we were kids, my parents bought a game called the *Ungame*.[3] It wasn't really a "game" in the true sense of the word.

It had zero competition and consisted of people taking turns asking each other questions, from a set of cards. Even though it sounded kind of boring, we grew to love it because it was really fun to answer the questions and to see how others would answer theirs!

As was confirmed in the Aron study we looked at in the last chapter, getting to know someone by asking them questions is one of the best ways to build closeness. Never assume that you know everything there is to know about the person who shares your bed and your home. Every person is an island to be explored!

Let's look at some fun ways to do just that. You can try most of these with the kids, too.

A. BUY THE *UNGAME* AT YOUR LOCAL GAMES STORE OR ONLINE. There are several different versions. A similar series of games is called *TableTopics.*[4]

B. DO THE 36 QUESTIONS CHALLENGE. THIS ONE *MIGHT* BE A BIT too intimate for stepfamilies, unless you already know each other well, but the questions are a wonderful way of building a sense of closeness between you and your spouse. Let yourself be flexible with this exercise – you might not have time to ask all the questions in one sitting. To find these questions online, search for "36 Questions" and you will find several sources where you can find the questions.

C. TRY THE "WOULD YOU RATHER," GAME. THIS INVOLVES GIVING the other person two alternatives to choose from, such as "would you rather go on an Alaskan cruise or a safari in Africa?"

. . .

ANOTHER VERSION OF THIS GAME IS THE "THIS OR THAT" GAME where a person asks their partner to choose between two things, such as "tea or coffee?" These questions can be as simple or as deep as you want them to be.

D. TRY A BOOK OF CONVERSATION STARTERS, WHICH GIVE conversation prompts to start things rolling.

E. DO A CONCENTRATED LISTENING TIME FOR EACH OTHER, where one person is allowed to talk freely for a specified period of time and the other one just listens and asks clarifying questions, without offering advice or opinions.

F. TAKE TIME, REGULARLY, TO SIMPLY HAVE CONVERSATION AND try to get to know each other, without talking about bills, kids or household duties.

LOOK AT EACH OTHER

In the last chapter, I shared how I tried staring into my husband's eyes for four minutes straight, like I had read about in the article. He looked up to see me staring intently into his eyes and got freaked out by it. I can see now how it must have looked kind of creepy! What I didn't tell you was that we tried it again later that night, with different results.

After I had filled him in on why I was staring at him like a crazy woman, we stared into each other's eyes for four minutes. At first, it felt kind of awkward and then it was nice, like some of the barriers started to break down.

How rare it is to *truly* look in each other's eyes these days! I encourage you to do more of it. There's nothing particularly special about the four-minute quota but the idea is to do it *some*. Look at each other, intently, instead of looking at the computer, at the television or at your smartphone.

GRAB A FEW MINUTES

You may have heard the advice, "go on a date once a week." Yeah, I have heard it, too, but guess what? We haven't always followed it. The weekly date is an excellent idea, if you can do it, but it is not always do-able. For those whose schedules don't allow you to get out once a week, I have an alternative and it's called "grab a few minutes."

How does this work? Simply find a few minutes here and there, whenever you can grab it and make it a mini-date. Sometimes, it might be fifteen minutes of coffee talk in the morning. Other times, it's a few minutes right before you go to sleep. And then maybe four hours on Saturday when you go out to run errands and really enjoy each other's company, stopping for a dessert or coffee on the way home.

Now *ideally*, it is nice if couples can go out once a week, but sometimes you just cannot do it and you shouldn't feel guilty about it if you can't. So, grab a few minutes together during these busy times. Go on dates when you can. This will help to strengthen your second marriage, and help you to stay together. Most of all, have fun!

On my website, Second Chance Love, I offer a

downloadable PDF with a list of fun ideas that couples can do with just a few minutes time. This mini-book, titled, *11 Ideas for Connecting With Your Spouse: When You Don't Have Time,* is available here:

http://secondmarriage.xyz/connection-ideas

MAKE SOME SWEET, SWEET LOVE

The long-running television show called *The Bachelor*[5] features 25 women competing for the attention of one man for the chance to possibly get engaged. One by one, the women are eliminated until there are only three left, all hoping and wishing to be the one that is chosen by the bachelor for possible marriage.

On the second last date, all the candidates are offered the option of "the fantasy suite," a room where they can invite the bachelor in and spent an intimate evening getting to know each other. It is never shown, but it is implied, that sex is a part of the deal on many of these special evenings.

The fantasy suite is presented as a way that the couples can get to know each but for the women that are not chosen, how painful it must be to give themselves to him and then see him engaged to another woman three weeks later.

Sharing your body in a sexual relationship is one of the most intimate things you can do. When the two of you are committed, the marriage bed can be a safe place for you both to show your acceptance and love of each other.

Sex is misused in our society but it is meant to be the highest bonding experience a committed couple can share. When you are trying to get close with your spouse, don't overlook this powerful way of drawing together. Men might be the ones who seem to crave sex more but it isn't just a *physical craving*. It is a deep need for both men *and* women.

The term "make-up sex" has entered popular vernacular as referring to making love after a fight or an argument. There is a truth to the adage that "make-up sex is the best sex." This is because making love is a way to re-bond after you have been torn apart from conflict and strife.

When you can connect physically, it also helps to draw you together emotionally. Dr. Aron's study confirmed that the couples who were most in love made were very sexually involved with one another, making love often.

In this chapter, we discussed four ways of connecting with your spouse: talking, eye contact, mini-dates, and making love. The final exercise is designed to bring you closer by asking questions.

"TEN QUESTIONS TO LOVE" EXERCISE

With your spouse, take turns asking the following questions one another. Do not make any comments. You may ask a question to clarify, such as "do you mean ..." or to better understand what your partner said, such as "why is that?" Do not interrupt your spouse. Listen while they are talking, without any distractions.

1. WHAT WAS THE HARDEST THING YOU DID TODAY?

2. WHAT WAS YOUR FAVOURITE PART OF LAST WEEKEND?

· · ·

3. WHAT IS YOUR FAVOURITE QUALITY ABOUT YOURSELF?

4. WHAT ONE THING WOULD YOU MOST LIKE TO CHANGE ABOUT yourself?

5. WHO IS YOUR FAVOURITE PERSON IN *MY* FAMILY, AND WHY?

6. WHAT IS THE BEST GIFT THAT YOU HAVE EVER RECEIVED?

7. WHAT WOULD YOU LIKE TO BE DOING IN FIVE YEARS?

8. WHAT WOULD YOU LIKE TO LEARN?

9. HOW ARE YOU FEELING RIGHT NOW?

10. HOW COULD I MAKE YOU HAPPIER THIS NEXT WEEK?

14

YOU'RE MY BEST FRIEND

66 There is nothing on this earth more to be prized than true friendship.

— THOMAS AQUINAS

One of the nicest compliments my husband has ever given me is "you're my best friend." These words are especially meaningful to me because of all that we had to go through to get to the point of friendship. To be called a "best friend" is an honour because, unlike family, we choose our friends. Friends are the people in our lives that we choose to spend time with, and to share our lives with.

According to the study on older passionate couples we just looked at in Chapter 13, friendship is a key factor in maintaining romance in a marriage. That's kind of a relief because we certainly can't focus on romance every second of every day.

Most of our minutes and hours are focused on the things we need to do to survive and take care of our family. We have housework, jobs, kids to raise. All of us have a to-do list, whether written down or in our heads, of things we want to get finished by the end of the day.

Having a friend to help us along the way is a great blessing. Having someone to laugh with and work with is a good foundation to carry us through the good times and the tough times. So, what exactly do we look for in a good friend?

GOOD FRIENDS ... SHARE THINGS IN COMMON

Angus and Betty Jones have very different personalities. Angus is bubbly and extroverted, while Betty is organized and reflective. She longs for quiet evenings at home, tending to her house and garden, while he seeks opportunities to get out and make friends. The two of them have learned to manage their differences and find the commonalities that bind them together.

For the last fifteen years, they have attended a small church that teaches the gospel and values they both believe in. As the years go by, both have found ways to serve in the church's ministries. Betty explains, "When we started to become more involved in the church, it helped. We prayed together, had devotions together. As we get older, we are starting to do missions."

A research survey[1] conducted by the Australia Council on Families confirmed that several studies show that shared values and a common sense of mission are one of the keys to long-term marriage success. Even if you and your mate don't have all the same interests, sharing *some* core values and a common purpose is helpful for creating a successful union.

For those of us in a second marriage, sharing common values and purpose is even more important because of all the things that have the potential of tearing us apart. Many of us have children coming and going from our home to the "other house." There are voices and memories from the past, from another marriage that ended in either death or divorce.

Sometimes there is a sense of feeling less or second, compared to the first wife, the first family. So many things can tear us apart. And it is for this reason that I strongly encourage those in a second marriage to find something that draws the two of you together.

One way to develop this shared sense of purpose is to take part in a project or activity that you can participate in together. My husband and I have three cats and these three girls have been something that we share. For the first year and a half of our marriage, my husband didn't care for the cats but he was finally won over, and now the cats are something that we love together, that we talk about together. We also love to walk through the forest near our home and soak in the beautiful scenery.

Everyone's common project or activity will be different. It could be anything: from doing community service together, to enjoying travel as a couple, to getting really excited about your favourite sports team. The key is that you find your commonalities and pursue them as a couple. Make it a priority.

The first law of motion states that things will keep moving in the same direction, unless something stops it. So it is with couples. We are either getting closer, or getting further apart.

So, find something that pulls you together as a couple, and even better, as a family.

GOOD FRIENDS ... LAUGH TOGETHER

There is nothing in the world like an evening spent with a good friend or friends, when you can laugh your head off and forget about your troubles. The ability to laugh together goes a long way when it comes to marriage relationships, too.

Elise and Alex Roca are another pair that seem like complete opposites. Elise has always been super-responsible and loves to plan ahead, while Alex tends to fly by the seat of his pants. He has a wide circle of friends, while Elise sticks to her close group. Through all their differences, though, Elise says that it is laughter that has held them together. She states, "We make each other laugh. We can be silly together. That's what we have, that's what we share."

Laughing together is a strong way to build your friendship. A shared sense of humour can be developed over time, too. When Vern and I first got married, we were both pretty tense and found it hard to laugh together. In time, though, we have developed a repertoire of inside jokes that we share. We have learned to make each other laugh, as we get to know one another better.

GOOD FRIENDS ARE ... LOYAL

When I was a student in university, I had a summer job working in the city municipal office. That year, I met some real interesting characters, many of whom were "lifers" -- they had worked in the office for over thirty years. Because they knew each other so well, their conversation was sometimes overly familiar.

I remember one man speaking about his wife and explaining very loudly how he couldn't stand to be with her. I was so shocked at the time to hear someone speak so poorly about someone he was married to, to his coworkers. What a terrible violation of trust.

Unfortunately, this happens far more often that it should. I have heard so many people speaking disparagingly of ones they love, to virtual strangers, about trivial matters.

Our media also encourages this type of behaviour. So many television shows and internet memes are based around a wife or husband making fun of their spouse, all for a good laugh. While it may be funny in a show, when it happens in real life, it is extremely harmful.

We would never knowingly stay friends with someone who talked about us behind our back. In the same way, we need to be loyal to our partner and not speak poorly about him to those around us. It is different if we speak confidentially to a friend or a counsellor to get some advice, but we should not bad-mouth our spouse to anyone.

GOOD FRIENDS ARE ... ACCEPTING

Years ago, I read an article in a Reader's Digest publication that talked about secrets to a happy marriage, and one of the secrets was that you should treat your husband like you would treat a stranger. That advice has always stuck with me because of how ironic it is that we are often nicer to strangers than we are to those in our own household.

Would we berate a stranger if she made a silly mistake?

Would we ignore a stranger when they tried to have a conversation with us? No, when we meet new people, we are on our best behaviour. We want to impress them as being decent human beings. If we were to take more of that attitude with our own spouse, how different we might treat them!

We are also often more accepting and kind to friends than we are to our spouse. It is not always easy to stay positive with our mate when we see the good, the bad and the ugly about them but we owe them at least that much.

This is where love comes in, the kind of love that is not romantic and gooey but tough. Strong enough to hold our tongue when our wife messes up. Robust enough to put up with our husband's annoying habits. Determined enough to stop yelling when we feel frustrated.

For Elise and Alex Roca, besides their shared sense of humour, it is also a deep sense of acceptance that binds them together. Elise tells how this feeling of being loved has helped to sustain their relationship:

I always asked God for someone to love me unconditionally. I thank God that Alex loves me. I never had that before. He accepts me for who I am. He tells me I am beautiful without make-up. It's very hard to find someone that accepts you like that.

REFLECTION QUESTIONS

1. Do you consider you and your spouse to be good friends? Why or why not?

2. USING A SCALE OF 1-5, HOW WOULD YOU RATE YOU AND YOUR spouse on the following characteristics of friendship?

a. Sharing things in common

b. Sharing laughter

c. Loyalty

d. Acceptance

3. WHICH ONE OF THE CHARACTERISTICS OF FRIENDSHIP, IF ANY, do you think needs the most work?

a. Sharing things in common

b. Sharing laughter

c. Loyalty

d. Acceptance

HANDLING CONFLICT

 Honest disagreement is often a good sign of progress.

— *MOHANDAS K. GANDHI*

During their first years of marriage, Betty and Angus Jones struggled with feeling depressed about their relationship. Angus tended to keep everything to himself and shut himself away, while Betty felt like she was constantly pursuing him to talk.

One of their most common disagreements concerned Angus's ex-wife. Because he did not want to make waves, Angus would often change plans concerning the children when his ex-wife requested it. He did not consult with Betty first but instead came home and informed her of the new schedule.

This did not go over very well with Betty. She would feel very frustrated and let Angus know, but he did not want to upset his former partner. To handle the escalating tension, Angus would shut himself away from his wife and find ways to get out of the house. This left Betty feeling alone and abandoned by her partner when she most needed his support.

Conflict is a part of every marriage and the complications of a second marriage make disagreements even more likely. Many of us can relate to the problems that the Jones had. It is hard negotiating with an ex-partner. It leads to power struggles and hurt feelings. We desperately need skills in navigating the conflict.

Angus and Betty were helped greatly when they both took some conflict resolution training at their jobs. The training helped them learn to handle their disagreements and helped save their marriage.

In this section, we will talk about some strategies for handling conflict I have learned from my own marriage, and from my years as a school teacher.

WE FIGHT BECAUSE ... WE FEEL LEFT OUT

I taught grade six for four years. My days were often filled with preteen conflicts, usually involving girls. Girls at this age are particularly skilled at letting other girls know who's *in* and who's *out*, without saying a word. An arched eyebrow can speak volumes and one girl is hurt by the other one silently signalling her disapproval. A student can feel bullied and ignored, even when no mean words have ever been spoken.

A big cause of conflict in marriage, especially second marriages, is that we feel left out. When our partner makes a decision without including us or seems to choose other things besides us, we feel left out of their life.

The stepfamily situation can really intensify these feelings. The parent has grown accustomed to making decisions with just herself and her children. She is not used to having to consult with another person and may not always think of communicating with her new husband concerning decisions regarding the kids.

As was the case with the Joneses, it is made even worse when the biological parent makes plans with their ex-partner concerning the children with no consultation with their wife or husband. The spouse is then forced to change her plans. Often, her anger is not so much at having to make the change, but at not being consulted.

If you are the one who feels left out, the key is to find a way to let your spouse know without becoming overbearing and accusatory. Calm down before you mention anything and try to say it in an honest way that communicates your needs. I have found that bringing things up in this manner has worked wonders in our marriage.

If you are the one who is leaving your mate out, try to be more sensitive to her feelings and honour her by including her in your decisions. Perhaps you are worried about your children feeling hurt, but this is part of the transition of moving from a single-parent home to a blended family.

As you move forward together as a family, you will begin to develop a new dynamic that will grow to become the norm. If you continue to leave your spouse out of decisions that affect her, you are putting your marriage at risk because the resentment can build up so strongly that the two of you become enemies.

WE FIGHT BECAUSE ... WE FEEL FRUSTRATED

All teachers know that students who struggle academically often end up having behavioural problems too. When a child feels frustrated that they can't do well at their schoolwork, many students take out their frustration on other students or by rebelling against authority.

Many disagreements in a marriage stem from feeling exasperated, too. If you or your spouse are frustrated, it is much more difficult to communicate in a polite way. When we feel like we can't change something, we feel a deep sense of disappointment and helplessness. The never-ending complications of a second marriage, with all the adjustments to make it work, are fertile grounds for frustration.

If you think your arguments are stemming from frustration, remind yourself that yelling at your spouse will not fix whatever issue is bothering you. In fact, yelling at someone is guaranteed to make it worse.

When you start to feel that tension building inside yourself, take a moment to ask what is *really* bothering you. Then, remind yourself that you really love your spouse, even if she is the one that is frustrating you right now.

WE FIGHT BECAUSE ... WE LACK COMMUNICATION SKILLS

Teaching students how to communicate better and to confront one another in a positive manner is one of the most important jobs of an elementary school teacher. Kids often don't realize that they can express their feelings without causing an argument. As teachers, we try to model these behaviours, along with teaching the skills overtly.

Marriages also suffer from poor communication skills. If, like me, you grew up listening to your parents fighting, it is programmed into you. When the pressure is on, we revert to what we learned subconsciously as children.

Learning to handle conflict productively is a skill that is invaluable in marriage and in all our relationships. In this next section, I will outline what I have learned over the years. Some of this is from my own marriage and my (many) mistakes. It is also from my years working as a teacher and handling conflict every day in the classroom. Here are the four principles:

1. Use good timing
2. Be positive
3. Don't belabour things
4. Don't defend yourself

Use good timing

One of the things I have learned is to bring things up at the right time. Before I learned this skill, I brought things up *whenever they crossed my mind* and this alone caused many a fight.

What I learned is that waiting for the right time can make the difference between a ten-minute civil discussion and a full-out drag-em-out war with my husband.

Good timing almost always leads to much better results. I can think of many occasions where we have had a terrible row and the next day, my husband would say, "Sorry I reacted that way. I was just tired. I really don't mind if you ..."

Timing is made even more difficult in a stepfamily situation because of the added complication of custody schedules. Trying to time your discussions when the kids are not there is challenging. You might have to wait until they are sleeping, but by then both of you may be too tired to talk.

For my husband and me, he works shift work, which makes it even harder. Finding the right time to bring up issues and talk about them can be extremely challenging. It will take perseverance, planning and patience. All this work, though, is worth it. Good timing can make all the difference.

When is the right time? It is a time when both of you are calm enough to talk about something rationally and without pressure. What is the wrong time? Here are some examples of the wrong time:

• Right when your sweet love is about to walk out the door

• Exactly as your spouse closes his eyes to go to sleep

• When the two of you are rushing about getting ready to go somewhere

• When the children are close by

So, we have established some bad times for bringing up difficult issues. What are some good times to talk to your spouse about something that is bothering you in your relationship? Here are some ideas:

• When the two of you are alone

• When you are staying home for the night

• When you are out together and having an enjoyable time

• When you have some time to talk about it

• When you are not too tired, stressed or hungry to be rational

Do you notice how the right time is always when you are both relaxed? Why is that? If you bring things up when you are stressed, hungry, exhausted, or in a hurry, you may say things that you regret. Your stress will be talking, instead of your rational calm mind, and this *often* leads to conflict.

Bring Things Up in a Positive Manner

When you have an issue to discuss, try to state it in a positive but firm way. If you are feeling angry, try to wait a few minutes, so that you make an effort to frame your communication in a more gracious manner. Being positive in your communication means focusing more on the desired outcome, and less on complaining about what *isn't* happening.

Here are some examples of the difference:

NEGATIVE: YOU NEVER THINK ABOUT ME WHEN YOU CHANGE our plans!

POSITIVE: I WOULD REALLY LIKE IT IF YOU ASKED ME BEFORE changing our plans.

NEGATIVE: WHY AM I THE ONLY ONE TO EVER DO ANYTHING around here?

POSITIVE: I COULD REALLY USE YOUR HELP WITH THE housework.

NEGATIVE: I AM SO SICK OF YOUR KIDS NEVER LISTENING TO ME

POSITIVE: I HAVE NOTICED THAT THE CHILDREN DON'T SEEM TO respect me.

. . .

Don't Belabour Things

One of the hardest things I had to learn in my marriage was to stop belabouring things. I used to refuse to let things go until an issue was one hundred percent solved. When I started to let things go more, my marriage got a whole lot better. I *finally* learned to bring something up once but then let it go if the conversation didn't go as planned.

Do you tend to belabour things? If you do, I encourage you that not everything has to be solved this very minute, this very hour, or even this very day. If something is bothering you, it is okay to bring it up once but then be willing to let it go if the conversation doesn't go exactly as you planned.

If you don't get what you want, bring it up again BUT wait for a while, like maybe a couple of days. And don't mention that you brought it up before. Act like it is something you have never said before.

Don't Defend Yourself

If you are the one who is being confronted, I encourage you to listen to what the other person is saying. Even if they say it in a way that you find hurtful, your spouse is giving you valuable information about his needs. If it makes you feel angry in return, try to wait a few minutes.

Now, this is the hardest part! Don't defend yourself! If you are tempted to defend yourself, I understand. For most of my life, I was the queen of defensiveness. But what I have finally learned, after many years, is that when you defend yourself, it is as if you haven't listened to a word your partner has just said. It appears as if you don't care. Instead, your sole purpose is to prove that you really are a good person and that you don't deserve to be confronted.

ENOUGH IS ENOUGH: ABUSE, ADULTERY & ADDICTIONS

The principles of this chapter apply to *most* situations but there are times when these principles won't be helpful until more serious issues are dealt with.

If you are dealing with abuse, adultery, or addictions, you need to get help that goes beyond the scope of this book. These problems are deal-breakers in a marriage and if not dealt with, will destroy both of you.

If there is physical abuse going on, your primary concern needs to be the safety of you and your children. You need to tell someone what is going on and get help.

If there is emotional abuse, you need counselling to help get through it and this issue is beyond the scope of this book. I come from a home where I witnessed verbal abuse regularly and experienced it my own marriages. I know that this is an issue where you need to talk to someone.

People can change their behaviour in this area, if they are willing to undergo counselling but sometimes they are not willing. If you are being belittled on a constant basis, this is not a situation that can be sustained.

You need help and I strongly suggest counselling to help you sort things out. Push for the other party to get counselling, too. Without counselling these patterns will continue and they are harmful for you, and for your children to witness.

If you or your partner have a serious addiction like drugs, alcohol or gambling, your marriage problems cannot be solved without addressing the addiction issues. This kind of relationship is not sustainable unless the addict admits the problem and gets help.

Finally, if you are dealing with adultery, you know this behaviour will have to change for the marriage to continue. Some people choose to walk away after an affair. Others choose to work it out. To work it out, though, there needs to be full confession and a complete change in behaviour. Like the other deal-breakers, you need professional help to deal with this kind of situation.

If you are in any of these situations, my heart goes out to you. Know that you are valuable and don't deserve to be treated in this way. It would take another book to address your concerns. At the end of this book is a section called "Recommended Resources." Check there for some resources for dealing with these very difficult issues. Most of all, I again encourage you to get help and reach out to talk to someone.

In this chapter, we have looked at some ways to better handle the inevitable conflicts that arise in our marriage by using better timing, a more positive approach and by letting things go. We have also examined a couple of reasons that people argue: because they feel left out and because they feel frustrated. This next exercise is designed to help you practise effective communication skills.

"TALK TO ME" EXERCISE

1. Write up to three things that are bothering you in your marriage right now. They could be trivial things or key issues.

· · ·

EXAMPLES MIGHT BE: HOUSEWORK ISSUES, MONEY PROBLEMS, discipline disagreements, ex issues, personality differences.

2. FOR EACH ISSUE, WRITE DOWN SOMETHING YOU MIGHT SAY (OR have said) to your spouse in anger or frustration, about this issue.

EXAMPLE: YOU ALWAYS WAKE ME UP WHEN YOU GET UP EARLY TO go to work! Don't you care that I need to get my sleep?

3. NOW, FOR EACH THING THAT YOU HAVE WRITTEN, WRITE A more positive way of saying this.

EXAMPLE: I JUST LOVE GETTING THAT EXTRA BIT OF SLEEP IN THE morning after you leave for work. Would you mind being a bit quieter, so I can indulge myself a little?

THE DANCE OF OPPOSITES

> Personality is to a man what perfume is to a flower.

> — CHARLES M. SCHWAB

*H*ave you ever wanted to scream because your partner just doesn't understand you? If you and your mate are complete opposites, don't despair. Help is on the way!

I am married to my opposite too. I used to desperately type "married to my opposite" and "incompatibility" into my search engine late at night, seeking answers from anyone who had a happy marriage, despite being different from their spouse in *every single way.*

Miraculously, I now consider these differences to be our greatest strength. For a long time, however, I believed these differences would be the end of us.

If you think you and your mate are incompatible, this chapter is for you. I have created a short four-part personality test, based on work from Carl Jung[1] to test how different or similar the two of you are. Throughout this chapter, as in the rest of the book, I have alternated between male and female pronouns. So, remember that these personality characteristics can be applied to both men and women.

WHEN YOUR PERSONALITY TYPES ARE THE SAME

When you take these mini-tests and find that you are the same in certain areas, know that these are your safe zones, the places where you naturally feel comfortable with one another.

When you share a personality trait with your spouse, you will find it easier to get along in these areas. You resonate with your partner. Treasure your similarities.

For example, two extroverts may especially enjoy going out and socializing together, or having guests over to their home. Two introverts, conversely, may especially relish quiet time over a weekend to read and snuggle in front of the fireplace.

Because the differences are what we find the most challenging, these differences are the primary focus of this chapter. If you would like to take these tests in an interactive form, they are also available in the free workbook, which is available at: http://secondmarriage.xyz/sign-free-resources-page.

A paperback version of the workbook should be available on Amazon, soon, as well.

EXTROVERT/INTROVERT DIFFERENCE

Personality Quiz #1

1. Which is truer of you?

a. I like my quiet time

b. I crave being around people

2. Which is truer of you?

a. I get stressed if I am around people too much

b. I get depressed if I am alone too much

3. Which is truer of you?

a. Large groups of people make me feel exhausted!

b. Large groups of people make me come alive!

IF YOU ANSWERED MORE A'S THAN B'S, YOU ARE AN INTROVERT. This means you primarily get your energy from being alone.

IF YOU ANSWERED MORE B'S THAN A'S, YOU ARE AN EXTROVERT. This means that you primarily get your energy from being around people.

ASK YOUR SPOUSE THESE QUESTIONS, OR ANSWER WHAT YOU think they would answer (if they won't do the questions with you.)

IF YOUR SPOUSE HAS MORE A'S, SHE IS AN INTROVERT.

. . .

IF SHE HAS MORE B'S, SHE IS AN EXTROVERT.

ANOTHER QUICK WAY TO DETERMINE IF YOU ARE PRIMARILY AN introvert or an extrovert is to ask the question: what would make me more tired, to be alone for three days in a row, without any interaction, or to be around people I don't know, for three days in a row?

If being alone for three days without interaction sounds like your worst nightmare, then you are probably an extrovert. This is very much my husband. When I used to work long hours at the school where I was a teacher, he started getting grouchy. It took a while for me to realize that it was because he was spending so much time alone. Too much time alone actually exhausted him.

An introvert's worst nightmare is to spend too much time with people she doesn't know. If you are an introvert, you physically *need* some quiet time alone to recharge your batteries.

An Introvert's Perspective

Second marriage can be especially difficult for the introvert because a stepfamily involves living with people (your stepchildren) that you don't really know that well. In time, you will, but at the beginning, you are all still struggling with how to *not* be strangers!

Don't feel guilty if it is hard to be around your stepkids sometimes. It doesn't mean you don't love them. Even biological mothers feel this way sometimes, towards their children. If you struggle with needing some more "alone time" than you are getting, don't waste time feeling guilty! Instead, make an effort to carve out some alone for yourself, so you are less grumpy.

If your spouse is an extrovert, he may not understand your need to spend time away from the kids, and perhaps, even away from him. He doesn't have that same need himself, and is perfectly happy with people around him at all times.

Because he doesn't understand something, he may interpret your actions to mean that you don't like his kids, or even him.

That is why it is very important to understand and communicate your differences with your spouse. If he is open, I would suggest even reading this portion of the book to him and saying, "This is me." Another way is to simply say at times, "It's just my introvert. I need some time alone. It's nothing against anyone."

For the first two years of our marriage, my husband was offended by my need for "alone time." He took it personally and concluded that I didn't care about the marriage or his kids. When he started to understand, and even celebrate that creative, inward part of me, things started to improve greatly.

An Extrovert's Perspective

If you are an extrovert married to an introvert, understand that your spouse needs some alone time and don't take it personally. She needs to wind down after a busy day by withdrawing into her own space, realize that it is a need, not just an excuse to be lazy!

Because you are an extrovert, you love being around people and can't understand the need for an introvert to get away. Know that your mate may find the constant pressure of children around her to be stressful. It doesn't mean she does not love them – it just means she can't take too much loud activity.

Pressuring an introvert to be more outgoing will only push them further into themselves. Don't interpret a partner's desire to stay home as rejection and a lack of caring.

Because you are the more outgoing partner, take the kids out for an activity when you sense your spouse needs some quiet time. You will love the excitement, and your spouse will greatly benefit from the "alone time" at home. Also, don't be afraid to go out with friends without your spouse sometimes. You have a genuine need for more socialization than your partner does and by going out, you will also be giving her some quiet time, which is a win-win for both of you!

Balancing the Differences

In conclusion, the introvert/extrovert difference can eventually be a great blessing for the relationship. The extrovert can take more of the socializing role in the relationship, sometimes shielding his partner from the demands of excessive visiting by doing it himself, while the introvert can help the extrovert to slow down and relax a bit.

SENSING/INTUITION DIFFERENCE

Personality Quiz #2

1. **Which is truer of you?**

a. You like talking about abstract ideas OR

b. You like talking about projects you are working on

2. **Which is truer of you?**

a. You prefer to read novels or books about ideas OR

b. You prefer to read how-to books

3. **Which is truer of you?**

a. You tend to not notice things as much as some people OR

b. You are pretty observant

IF YOU ANSWERED MORE A'S THAN B'S, YOU ARE MORE ON THE intuitive side. This means you are more into ideas than practicality.

IF YOU ANSWERED MORE B'S THAN A'S, YOU ARE MORE ON THE sensing side. This means that you are more practical than intuitive.

ASK YOUR SPOUSE THESE QUESTIONS, OR ANSWER WHAT YOU think they would answer (if they won't answer.)

IF YOUR SPOUSE HAS MORE A'S, SHE IS MORE INTO IDEAS THAN practicality.

If he has more b's, he more sensing than intuitive.

THIS PERSONALITY FUNCTION IS RELATED TO HOW YOU AND YOUR spouse see the world. Do you get your information about the world primarily through your five senses, or do you tend to rely more on your intuition?

A Sensing Perspective

If you are a sensing person, you see the world in a more realistic manner. You worry more about what "is" rather than thinking about what "could be." You might say things like "let's get real" or "that's just the way it is." You feel impatient with people who seem to be too vague or dreamy.

As a sensing person, you probably excel at hands-on activities such as handyman (or woman) work or gardening. You probably don't care too much for theoretical discussions.

If you are a sensor and your partner is not, you may sometimes feel frustrated that he is less observant than you are. It is possible that you think that he wastes too much time on things that are *not real* and neglects some of the practical tasks that need to be done.

An Intuitive Perspective

If you are an intuitive person, you may have been accused once or twice of having your head in the clouds. You interpret the world more through a "gut feeling" or "sense." You may tend to be less naturally observant in every day life and not always notice things that other people notice. You may make decisions that other people don't necessarily understand, based on "just a feeling."

As an intuitive person, your sensitivity is your strength. If you are intuitive and your partner is a sensor, you may feel misunderstood in your desire to talk about abstract matters. You may also be impatient with the other person seeing only what's in front of her. You may feel that your world is misunderstood by your partner.

These Differences Can Be Your Strength

If you and your partner are opposites in this area, believe that in time, these differences can be a blessing. The sensing partner can help the more intuitive partner deal with reality better and keep them on track for what needs to be done. The intuitive partner can help their spouse to see beyond the grindstone and have more vision for the future.

One of my favourite television shows is *Fixer Upper*[2] on HGTV. Chip and Joanna Gaines work out of Texas making beautiful dream homes from outdated, ugly houses. I am not sure of what personality types they are, but going by what I have seen on the show, they seem like a sensor and an intuitive.

Joanna is the visionary of the two. She decides how a place will be turned from a dump into a mansion. "Tear a wall down here," and "add a gazebo here." Then, after Joanna puts her plan on paper and gets approval from the homeowners, Chip makes it happen.

He says his favourite day is demolition day and he obviously enjoys getting those walls down, tearing out those ugly cupboards and getting things ready to build. The result is always spectacular and both were needed to get it done.

This duo is a notable example of how a sensing and an intuitive couple can work together to make things happen.

THINKING / FEELING DIFFERENCES

Personality Quiz #3

   1. Which is truer of you?
   a. You love to figure out the plot of a movie OR
   b. You love to analyze the motives of a movie character
   2. Which is truer of you?
   a. I don't usually take things personally OR
   b. I tend to take things personally
   3. Which is truer of you?
   a. My decisions are rarely affected by my emotions OR

b. My decisions are often affected by my emotions

IF YOU ANSWERED MORE A'S THAN B'S, YOU ARE MORE OF A thinker.

If you answered more b's than a's, you are more of a feeler.

ASK YOUR SPOUSE THESE QUESTIONS, OR ANSWER WHAT YOU think they would answer (if he won't take part.)

IF YOUR SPOUSE HAS MORE A'S, HE IS MORE OF A THINKER.

If he has more b's, he is more of a feeler.

THIS PERSONALITY FUNCTION RELATES TO HOW YOU MAKE decisions. Do your choices depend more on feelings or on logic? Another way to tell what type you are is to ask, when you meet someone, is your first instinct to wonder how they are feeling or do you analyze their words to see if they make sense? All of us use both logic and have feelings but this personality difference has to do with which we use first: feelings or logic.

The Thinker's Perspective

First, if you are a thinker in this personality test, it doesn't mean that you don't have feelings. It just means that you tend to use logic *first* when you make decisions. You want to be fair and impartial and make sure that you are not biased by feelings, when you shouldn't be. You believe in feelings but think that they should be kept in their proper place.

If you are married to your opposite, you may feel like your spouse tends to be too emotional and not see the truth as it is. You may feel frustrated when your spouse says things that don't really make sense to you. Because you don't understand him, you may tend to discount what he says. Let's be honest – his lack of logic may even cause you to disrespect him sometimes.

But as the more logical spouse, know that your partner does use logic – it is just after he processes his feelings first! Give your partner time to work through his feelings and respect his process. Then, he will be ready to listen to your logical arguments. Take time, though, to also listen to the more feelings-based arguments that your partner puts forth. He will probably point out things that you haven't taken notice of.

For example, you may want to enter a business deal but your mate doesn't think it's a good idea. There's a good chance that he notices something in the way the person involved conducts himself. Because he is more skilled at noticing feelings, he will be more aware of how to read other people's emotions and trustworthiness.

The Feeler's Perspective

If you are the more feeling one in your marriage, try not to take it personally if your spouse is not as emotional as you are. She is not built that way but it's okay because she has other strengths that probably benefit you.

If your partner is thinking-based, she may be stricter with the children than you. She is probably very concerned that the children understand and follow the rules that help society function. A thinking-oriented partner is good at helping the children to learn discipline and to follow goals.

If your children are used to your style, as a feeler, and your partner is the stepparent, be careful before you hand over the reigns to her. Because your children are used to your more personal approach, they might really buckle under the less personal style of the thinker.

If you have disagreements on how to raise the children, try to take some time away from the house and hammer out some of the expectations that both of you have.

These Differences Can be Your Strength

How do these differences affect a marriage? As with all the functions, we can sometimes judge our partner's actions according to our own personality and assume our partner is doing things with a bad motive. As we have said before, our differences in this area can be a true gift.

If you are the feeler, your partner can help give you another perspective besides your own. I am a feelings-based person and I know that I can let my emotions get in the way of taking a firm stand on something.

A thinker spouse can help you to make tough decisions. When my husband and I first got started talking on the phone, he told me that he wasn't very emotional. It took me a long time to accept that this was actually a bonus for me.

My less emotional partner now supports me and helps me to see a more logical solution when my emotions are too strong for me. I am grateful for our differences!

If you are the thinker partner, be grateful for your feeler partner. She notices things that you don't. By listening to her insights, you can save yourself a world of trouble. Your feeler spouse is especially good at seeing how the children are doing and making sure they are emotionally healthy.

Remember that as a couple, this difference can be your

greatest strength, as you work together and take advantage of your two different perspectives.

THE STRUCTURED/OPEN-ENDED DIFFERENCES

Personality Quiz #4

    1. Which is truer of you?

    a. I tend to plan everything carefully

    b. I tend to go moment by moment

    2. Which is truer of you?

    a. I tend to keep my things neat and tidy

    b. I struggle with being messy

    3. Which is truer of you?

    a. I am usually a bit early

    b. I am often running late

IF YOU ANSWERED MORE A'S THAN B'S, YOU ARE MORE structured.

If you answered more b's than a's, you are more open-ended.

ASK YOUR SPOUSE THESE QUESTIONS, OR ANSWER WHAT YOU think they would answer (if they don't wish to take part.)

IF YOUR SPOUSE HAS MORE A'S, HE IS MORE OPEN-ENDED.

IF HE HAS MORE B'S, HE IS MORE STRUCTURED.

. . .

THIS PERSONALITY FUNCTION HAS TO DO WITH HOW STRUCTURED a person is in his behaviour. Another way to tell if you are structured or open-ended is to ask yourself. Do you prefer finishing a project or starting a project? How much does it bother you if things are still "in process?"

The structured person really likes to get things done. He does not enjoy the process as much as the end goal. An open-ended person gains a great deal of pleasure from the process itself and is less concerned about being finished. Of course, we all enjoy the process of doing things and we all like getting things done, but this is about which one we like better!

The Structured Person's Perspective

If you are more of a structured individual, it will really bother you when things are left undone around the home or at work. You most likely have a to-do list and one of your greatest pleasures is ticking off those boxes.

If your partner is more open-ended, you may feel frustrated with her not always getting chores done on the schedule that you would prefer. One way to encourage your more open-ended spouse is to focus less on them doing things exactly according to *your* schedule.

Try to give them more freedom about *when* things need to be done and appreciate what they *are* doing. Your encouragement and praise will go much further than nagging if things are not completed perfectly.

Another area of potential conflict for you, as a couple, is getting to events on time. If punctuality is very important to you and your spouse doesn't value it as much, you may end up fighting over this issue. Try to not treat your spouse like a child and let him handle this area of his life. You might even consider going in different vehicles, if that is possible.

The Open-Ended Person's Perspective

If you are more of an open-ended person, you enjoy the process of starting tasks more than you do finishing them. You would probably prefer to start a business, with all the excitement of getting things off the ground than you would to run the business from day-to-day. You like some variety in your life and find it hard to keep to the grind of doing the same thing day after day.

Because your partner is so different from you, perhaps you feel hemmed in and not accepted by her. Maybe you feel controlled by your spouse's rules and expectations. You may long for adventure, while your more structured partner feels these types of pursuits are frivolous and not worthy of spending time or money on.

Try to remember that your spouse has a need for getting things done in a timely manner. It's how she functions. If you are more relaxed, try to please her in some areas that are important to her.

Compromising

In this area, as in all the others, these differences can be a gift. The more structured partner can learn to have more fun and expand beyond her tight schedule, while the open-ended partner can learn to be stricter in certain areas of his life and be able to accomplish more, with more discipline.

The open-ended partner may have a greater sense of spontaneity with the children, while the more structured partner may prefer more routine for the child. This is an area where you are going to have to compromise. I would suggest trying to hammer out an agreement at a place away from the house, where you can talk about your areas of disagreement and work something out that suits both of you.

I will give you an example of a couple I know well. I will call them Jake and Lori. Before they got married, Jake was very relaxed in his approach to life. He was very responsible at work but when he came home, he would spend most of his time watching television in his sweats. He dressed very casually and once or twice even wore sweats and a t-shirt to work.

Lori, on the other hand, was the opposite. She was very particular about her dress, had very little unscheduled time and was constantly working on her long to-do list. She was a hard worker and was known for being a bit too serious. When Lori and Jake first started dating, Lori was bothered by Jake's super casual approach toward life.

Lori and Jake have been married for 17 years now and it is remarkable to see the changes in both of them! After marrying Lori, with some gentle wardrobe advice, Jake started dressing more sharply. He was promoted at work several times and now holds one of the top jobs at his organization.

Through the loving acceptance and quiet ways of Jake, Lori is a much more relaxed person. She still likes to get things done, but also loves spending time hanging out with her kids. When the two of them first had children, she would get tense when the children did not follow her rules but she has learned to go with the flow.

Jake and Lori are an example of a couple who have made their differences a great strength.

CONCLUSION

In conclusion, personality differences are a reality in most marriages. None of us are exactly the same and we must deal with differences between us, whatever they are. It is true that opposites often attract and that is because we seek out whatever is missing in ourselves.

This is a long-term process but the two of you are learning from each other, even if you don't realize it. Let me give you an example. Let's say you're a cheapskate and your husband is a spendthrift. He is teaching you to be more generous and you are teaching him to be more disciplined. If she is a homebody and you are a social butterfly, she is teaching you to be more reflective and you are helping her to come out of herself.

When you and your partner butt heads over an area where you are opposites, remember that these differences can eventually be your greatest strength but it won't happen overnight. It will take an understanding that your spouse is different from you – not wrong. It will take a lot of communication to appreciate where your partner is coming from, and it will take compromise to find ways to live, so that both of you can co-exist together happily!

V

HEALING YOUR FAMILY

This next part of the book looks at healing your new stepfamily, if you have children. We will examine why second marriage is hard on kids, and what we can do to make it easier for them. I also address those who become parents for the first time by marrying someone else with children. If your second marriage does not involve children, skip ahead and go to the next section, "Taking Care of Yourself."

BECOMING A FAMILY

 Children are our most valuable resource.

— HERBERT HOOVER

*B*efore we got married, I asked Vern's youngest son for permission to marry his father. This twelve-year-old boy told me, "I am the kind of person who thinks people should be able to marry whoever makes them happy. So, as long as you make my Dad happy, I don't mind."

I thought that was remarkably mature and generous for a young guy, because accepting a new woman into their father's life isn't always easy for kids. Sure, *we* are excited about the new nuptials – the chance for a clean slate and a new chapter. But the children are usually not nearly as excited as we are.

In our enthusiasm for this new phase, let us not forget the delicate feelings of the little people in our lives. It is not as exciting for them, as it is for you. Let's try to see things from the child's perspective.

No matter how fond these stepchildren may be of their new stepparent, they are now forced to let go of the dream of their parents reuniting. Many children secretly dream of their parents getting back together, someday, somehow. Now that the two of you are married, that dream is dead.

The child may have thought her old family wasn't too bad, before it fell apart, much beyond her control. Before she has even been able to process *that* change, there is a now a new family to deal with.

So, be patient with your child. Part of him is probably grieving. Your remarriage (and new family) has *officially* ended the old family. Even if the divorce happened years ago, without a new marriage, there may have always been a slight possibility that his parents would get back together.

For the children of the widowed, their other parent is gone forever and adjusting to a new person in their life can be overwhelming. So, be patient with the children in your new marriage. Don't be surprised if they act out. Look for signs of grieving.

In this chapter, I won't be getting into too many of the details of my own stepfamily situation. I can say that I have two stepsons. They were 13 and 15 when my husband and I got married. We had custody every other weekend and sometimes we did extra evenings and longer periods of time. Two years into our marriage, the custody arrangements changed and we had full-time custody of Vern's youngest son.

As a family, we did have our share of disagreements, heartbreak and conflict. Lots of it. I can't share the exact details. They are not mine to share. Instead, I will share some of the lessons that I learned along the way. I will also share the true stories of men and women who agreed to open up with their struggles.

I also freely admit that I made *many* mistakes, especially during my first years of being a stepmom. I also did some things right. For the most part, I just muddled along and tried to survive. I don't have the answers to all the stepfamily issues in the world but I will share the things I have learned.

CUSTODY IS DIFFICULT

If you or your spouse's marriage ended because of divorce, and there were children involved, then you are involved in a custody situation. I don't have to tell you that custody is hard.

Custody means that you are granted the right to see your children at certain times by the court, and that care of your children is shared with an ex-partner. Custody is one of the most hurtful consequences of divorce, for children and parents alike because it is the separating of children between two homes, when they had been used to one home.

Children must constantly adjust. The children will come and go from your home and be forced to live in two places, where rules, customs and the general atmosphere will be different. How different they will be varies widely from situation to situation. Children will have to adjust *every time* they make the transition from Mom's place, to Dad's place, and back again.

It is not good for the parents, either. Whether you are the custodial or non-custodial parent, you don't have your children full-time. You wonder how the kids are doing during their time away from you, and you are constantly adjusting too. The child's other house now has a major influence on your home.

Custody is far from the ideal situation for everyone involved but it is a necessary evil that we are forced to deal with. This next section will deal with things that you can do to make custody easier on everyone involved.

UNDERSTANDING HIDDEN ROUTINES

When my husband and I first got married, I made a special kind of Kraft Dinner™ for the kids, with extra cheese and sour cream. I thought it tasted pretty good but they were not too impressed. However, when their Dad made his special "cheesy mac," that was special! You see, their father making this special food was one of their routines.

Even though I was a pretty decent cook, it wasn't the same unless Dad made it. Eating Dad's food was one of their routines. He had a way of doing it the same every time. I didn't realize it was a routine. Their Dad probably didn't even realize that "cheesy mac" was a routine, but the kids knew it was.

The little family that I entered had other hidden routines too. Playing video games all day on a Saturday. Going to MacDonald's every Thursday for Root Beers and Big Mac's. Wrestling one another to the ground wherever they went. My problem was that I didn't always see the routines, and when I did, I thought some of them should go.

I didn't particularly care for the routine where they played video games for twelve hours straight. I was concerned about their health, and I didn't care for the living room being completely tied up the entire day. I tried to change it, but it wasn't very well-received -- by my husband or the children.

My mistake was that I tried to change things too quickly. Instead of being a quiet influence, I got offended and started to complain to my husband about the terrible habits the boys were developing.

My approach failed miserably. Instead of them immediately seeing the error of their ways and deciding to have a nice balanced day of different activities, it caused tension. My husband thought I didn't accept the kids. It made him feel like I was calling him a bad father.

When a stepfamily is formed, it is formed by taking two families and joining them together. Sometimes it is two families with children, where they are forced to be stepbrother and sister. Other times, as in our case, the stepfamily is formed by a single person (me) entering a family with kids.

Whenever these two families come together to form a new family, there is going to be friction. Both parties are used to their family customs. I was used to my custom of having a quiet Saturday of relaxation before heading back to work. The noise of video games in the living room seemed intolerable.

For their family, the weekend was a time to relax and unwind. School was done for the week and they were enjoying their freedom.

It was all about fun. Their Dad was there to be goofy with him and keep them safe. They didn't want any structure messing up their day.

Neither family's routines were wrong. I wasn't wrong to want some quiet on a Saturday. The boys weren't wrong to want to be free on a Saturday. We were just different and we couldn't both have our Saturday tradition.

When you formed your new family, you have had to decide who gets to keep what traditions. The best way is if both parties get to keep some of their traditions, so that both families feel valued by the other side.

What happens often, though, is that these issues are never discussed. Instead, people give in and then feel resentful towards the partner who is getting their way. We acquiesce quietly until suddenly, there is a blow-up. We are tired of compromising – this is our house, too!

Blending two families together is like the merging of two companies. When two firms are joined together, they must decide which customs from either company will stay on and which customs will go out the door.

TAKE CHANGE SLOWLY

I see now that it would have been much better to learn to accept the culture of the family that I had just joined and then to quietly assert my influence as I got to know them better.

Taking change slowly is a good principle for building your new family. The remarriage itself is already a huge change for the children. In some cases, the marriage has also led to a move to a new house. The kids are adjusting to living with a new person or people.

Therefore, maintaining as many routines as possible, will help them a great deal. In the case of a single person joining a family with children, the adult should be the one to adjust to the other family's culture to start with. In some ways, I did this when my husband and I were married. Although I complained about my Saturdays, there were many other areas where I let things slide and kept my ideas about raising children to myself. I tried to respect their ways but sometimes I didn't, as I mentioned earlier.

Like a traveller surveying a new land, we need to observe the customs of this strange new territory, and then try to blend in. Once we are trusted occupants who have demonstrated that we are not there to take away all of the family's traditions, we can start to give suggestions and make our influence known. To step in too soon will often cause resentment and make the kids feel like everything in their life before didn't matter.

If you are the biological parent, be sensitive to your kids and their need to keep a lot of things the same, but also be open to your spouse's ideas. Don't dismiss his needs and desires, for the sake of the children.

Explain to your spouse the reasons that you want to take things slow. Don't get angry that your mate has an unique way of doing things. He is adding to your life and with any new growth, there is change. Take things slow, for their sake, but don't push your spouse away while you are doing it. Try to make those changes together.

DEVELOP NEW ROUTINES

As you grow together as a family, new routines will arise naturally. You will start to emerge into certain patterns and do things at certain times. Be glad for these new routines and make note of them with the children.

Say things like, "We always have a late dinner on Wednesday, don't we?" or "We always watch a movie on Friday nights!" Acknowledging the patterns forming in your lives together will bring a sense of family.

When my husband and I first started dating, all four of us used to go to Dairy Queen almost every weekend. It was quite the trek and it involved lots of talking and joking and of course, some wrestling. (It was three males, after all!) We usually all got Peanut Buster Parfaits.

This wasn't great for my waistline but it was wonderful for getting to know the boys. It was fun and the youngest one usually complained that the walk was too long. We didn't talk about anything serious but just being together was awesome.

This became a routine for us, one that drew us together. After we got married, we developed some new routines. They weren't big things but they were things that *we* did. I encourage you to draw out the small things that you are already doing and acknowledge them as routines. Don't go too fast. If you are the stepparent, try to be a quiet influence at first and then slowly introduce your ideas.

TAKE TIME TO LAUGH

With his goofy sense of humour, my husband has an innate gift for making *any* outing into something fun. I remember one trip to a department store while we were waiting to get our income taxes done. With anyone else, it would have been boring but he managed to entertain his youngest son in *The Bay* for almost two hours while I went shopping for clothes.

When I came out of the dressing room, they both approached me with some kind of weird kitchen gadget. "We need this," the boy exclaimed. Then they proceeded to tell me all the bizarre uses for this silly product, none of which were its intended use.

This ability to make any day a fun day is a gift that my husband has, and we can all learn from it. One of the best ways to bond together as a new family is to have fun together.

Kids need fun. When you are laughing, you are not focused on stress or conflict.

If you are the stepparent, don't let your spouse have all the fun, either. Let the kids know you as a person, not just as a role. You will get to know their goofier side, too!

GET INVOLVED AS MUCH AS POSSIBLE

Studies show that historically, children from stepfamilies, on average have suffered more social problems, behavioural issues and academic concerns. These studies have shown that stepchildren spend less time with their parents and receive less attention than children in homes where there are two biological parents.[1]

The best way to help your children not become part of these statistics is stay deeply involved in everything they are doing and show interest in whatever they are interested in.

Even though Angus Jones no longer shared a home full-time with his children, he did not let that stop him from being deeply engrossed in his children's activities. Jones explains:

> Every time they did something, we were involved. Whether it was band, baseball or camp, I was helping out with leadership and volunteering. Even their mother acknowledged that I was a good father. In any activity, I would be playing a major role in that activity.

To conclude, in this chapter we have learned that forming a stepfamily is like merging two businesses. Some practices have to go and some get to stay. Look for the traditions that are already there in each family and then try to develop new ones together.

"BACK IN THE OLD ROUTINE" EXERCISE

1. Do you have any routines with the children now? If so, what are they?

2. ASK THE CHILDREN WHAT THEY THINK YOUR FAMILY'S ROUTINES are. Write down what they say.

3. ASK THE KIDS WHAT NEW ROUTINES THEY WOULD LIKE TO develop as a family. It could be something serious or super-goofy. The important thing is that you do it together! Write it down here.

18

BECOMING A PARENT BY MARRIAGE

66 Don't feel guilty if you don't immediately love your stepchildren as you do your own, or as much as you think you should.

— JOHANN WOLFGANG VON GOETHE

*I*f you became a stepparent when you married your spouse, this chapter is for you. Becoming a parent to someone else's children is one of the hardest jobs in the world. It is usually thankless and when you mess up, your mistakes are noticed. When you do things right, no one seems to see it.

As a fellow stepparent, my heart goes out to you. I see your acts of love, so often unnoticed. You try to do the right thing, day in and day out. I see your frustrations. Please know you are not alone. You probably feel like you are – but you're not.

Stepparents are often the quiet backbone of the family, quietly offering support when needed and giving love without expecting much back. As the stepmom, you do the work of a mother but you probably won't get a Mother's Day card. As the stepdad, you make your home more secure, but you probably aren't fully trusted.

Being a stepparent is an act of faith. You put the work in now and believe that the investment will pay off down the road. The love you give will be built into your stepchildren's life and will show in a more healthy and accepted child and a bonded family later on.

But in the meantime, it's tough! As one stepparent to another, I understand. In this chapter, we will talk about why it's so difficult and how to better understand our role. Then, we will go over three ways to connect with your stepchildren.

NO RESUME REQUIRED: WHY IT'S SUCH A HARD JOB

Our last interview couple is John and Rachel Martens. This forty-something couple have been married for fifteen years now. John is a proud craftsman who runs his own business doing metalwork for high-end clients. Rachel works at a non-profit company and sells Etsy crafts on the side.

Rachel was 26 years old when she married her husband, John Martens. Before moving in with her husband, she was living with her parents and had her own independent life.

When she first married John, his children came over part-time during the week. Within two years of being married, the biological mother of her stepchildren moved in with a new boyfriend and decided she couldn't take care of the kids anymore.

This 28-year-old woman was suddenly the full-time mom to three children: aged 17, 10 and 11. Becoming a mom was a shock, to say the least. Rachel shares:

> *Here I was at age 28, and mom to three children, and I was doing it all. Cooking, laundry, everything. I felt lonely, like I was just a maid. I started to wonder why I had come here.*

It is easy for us to relate to Rachel. Becoming a stepmom is difficult because you are taking on the parenting of someone else's children, often against the child's will. They certainly didn't ask for a stepparent!

In many ways, becoming a stepparent is the opposite of becoming a parent. The problem is, we try to use the same methods and expect to get the same results. Here are four ways that being a parent is different than being a stepparent:

• A parent has a long history with his children. A stepparent has very little history with the children.

• A parent is recognized by society as the caregiver of her child. The stepparent is often not recognized by society as the caregiver of the child.

• The parent is perceived by the child as giving him everything he needs to live (food, clothing, shelter, love, entertainment). The stepparent is often perceived by the child as taking something from him – the attention of his parent. (When you get married, the child often sees you as taking time away from the time he spends with his mom or dad.)

• The common image of a parent is of a loving, benevolent

person. The stereotype of a stepparent is one of evil. (The "evil stepmother" is a character found in fairy tales such as Cinderella and Snow White.)

So, you can see why being a stepparent is difficult. You are trying to fulfill that parental role but without the automatic respect that is awarded the biological parent. Sometimes, like Rachel, you are the primary caregiver while your spouse goes to work, so you have no choice but to act as a parent.

LOYALTY BIND: I SHOULDN'T LIKE YOU BUT I DO

When I worked in a classroom with at-risk youth, most of the students in my class were from homes where the original parents were not together. They would often talk about their stepmom or dad with great disdain and disrespect, while they were longing for their biological parent who had often abandoned them for alcohol or drugs.

Sometimes being a stepparent can be very confusing because it seems like the kids like you one minute but then the next minute, they don't. You question yourself and ask, "what did I do wrong?" In order to stop taking this behaviour so personally, it is important to understand something called the "loyalty bind."

This is a term used to describe the way that a child feels a conflict of loyalties between his biological parent and his new stepparent. He may feel that liking, or showing kindness to the stepparent is, in fact, being disloyal to his own biological parent.

In some cases, the ex-partner will encourage their child in this feeling, and deliberately try to pit her child against the stepparent. In some cases, the ex uses this sense of loyalty bind to her advantage, making the child feel even guiltier if he likes the new partner, and the children feel like they have to please their parent.

The loyalty bind can even be felt when kids feel like they must pick between their mother and father. Angus Jones believes that his kids felt like they had to choose between liking him and liking their mother. This can delve into the realm of parent alienation, where a child is made to feel, by the ex-partner, that their mom or dad is "no good," and are kept away from their parent.

These situations are extremely heart-breaking and so harmful to both the parents and children. If you find yourself in this kind of situation, I recommend an excellent Facebook group called *A Family's Heartbreak . . . Parental Alienation.*

UNDERSTAND YOUR ROLE

If you are the stepparent, your role is confusing. On one hand, you know you aren't the children's biological dad or mom but on the other hand, you are often doing everything that a parent does: driving them places, feeding them, playing with them and sending them to bed.

Which is it? Are you a parent or not? You play a parental role, but you are not their *Mom or Dad.* At times you may feel like their Mom or Dad and even start thinking that you are, but you must be careful to remember that they already have or have had (in the case of a widowed parent) a mom or dad. You cannot become that person, just by marrying their parent. Your relationship *may* grow to the point where they take you as a parent, in time, but it has to be the children who want it, and you cannot force the issue.

Ideally, the biological parent would always take care of discipline but this is not always realistic. As a stepmom or dad, there will be times when you are left with the children and must be the adult in that situation. You will have to discipline and enforce boundaries. In our situation, my husband works shift work and so I was often left with the care of the boys. I had to have the authority when I was the only grown-up present.

This was awkward, though, because I was very aware of my lack of history with them. I knew I wasn't their mom but I had to act like I was. In our case, the boys were already teenagers, so I did not have to micromanage their every move, but they still had to respect a curfew and listen to house rules.

When it comes to discipline, you can't always rely on your spouse to do it. There are times when you are the adult in the room and you have to be the one that lays down the rules. Try to do it with as little drama as possible. Be confident or the kids will see right through you and may try to manipulate the situation to make you feel guilty.

If the biological parent has passed away, or is out of the picture due to negligence or moving far away, you may indeed take the role of parent on. I also know cases where the other parent had nothing to do with his son, and the stepdad became the father for that child, in almost every sense of the word.

Whatever the situation, it is true for all stepparents that relationships speak far louder than trying to impose your authority on the children. The more you get to know your step kids, the more they will show you the respect you long for. This next section gives three powerful strategies for connecting with your spouse's children, no matter their age.

LISTEN

Do you struggle with connecting with your stepchildren? This is one of the biggest challenges of a stepparent: developing a relationship with the children. One thing that really helped me connect with one of my stepchildren was to listen.

Listening with an unbiased ear is a great gift and really helps to bond with someone. Listen without judging and try to be real with him. The more genuine you are with your stepchildren, the more your relationship will grow.

Spend time having conversations. Get to know them -- their opinions and their interests. There is no shortcut for getting to know someone. You must put in the time. Conversation is an art and you share this art with them.

You don't have to necessarily agree with everything they say because that will make you sound insincere. Don't be scared to challenge them sometimes and question what they say. They will enjoy that you are being real. Don't act like you know everything – be curious and open for what they can teach you.

If the kids are teens, you might try to be a little sarcastic with them. Teenagers appreciate a little bit of sarcasm, as long it doesn't have a mean twist. Just asking questions and getting to know them is good. The more time you take to get to know them, the more likely they will begin to accept you when you are forced to play a disciplinary role.

"DO STUFF" TOGETHER

In our last chapter, we also talked about how having fun together is another awesome way of bonding with the whole

SHARILEE SWAITY

family. Besides going for outings, a profound way to connect
with the children in your life is to simply do everyday things
together. This may already be a natural part of your routine,
and if so, that's great!

If not, then start looking for opportunities to go out and do
activities with your stepchild. Take a walk to the store together.
Do the dishes. Watch a television show together. Offer to play
a video game with her. Whatever it is, the key is that you are
doing something together. A shared activity takes your mind
off the awkwardness of not knowing each other that well and
frees the two of you to just enjoy each other's company.

I am grateful to my husband who saw the need for shared
activity before I did. He constantly suggested that the youngest
son (who lived with us for two years) and I do things together.
He would drop the two of us off at the grocery store and say,
"You guys get some food and I'll be back in half an hour after I
get the oil changed." He saw the need for us to spend time
together, in order to bond, and took action to make it happen.

When you are doing "life" together, it is a fantastic
opportunity to get to know the children. Ask simple questions
that are not threatening and listen. Share some of your life
with them and relate to them without being too overbearing.
Just show that you are genuinely interested.

Next, we are going to look at one last way that you can
connect with your stepchildren: by honouring their
relationship with both parents.

HONOUR THE RELATIONSHIPS WITH THEIR PARENTS

When a stepmom or dad enters the picture, one of the child's biggest fears is that this man or woman will take away his parent. One way to earn the deep trust of your stepchild is to show them, with your actions, that you are not there to get in between her and your spouse. You are also not there to try to replace her *other* parent, either. Instead, you support both of them.

By supporting both parents (your spouse and her ex) you are demonstrating something very powerful to your child: that you are a peacemaker. That she doesn't have to *choose!* She can love you and love her other parent. That you will not try to limit her time with your spouse. By doing this, you will be dispelling the fear of the evil stepmother. The evil stepmother is jealous and wants the children destroyed, so she has her husband's love and attention all to herself.

How do you show your stepkids that you support both of her parents? Here are two powerful ways.

1. **Never talk poorly of their mom or dad:** Don't ever put their mother or father down. Only say good things about their parent, and if you can't do that, don't say anything at all. You may need to vent sometimes, behind closed doors, when the child is not around, but never let that spill over to where the child can see it.

2. **Encourage the child to spend time alone with your spouse:** Encourage your husband or wife to have time alone with their children, without you. Yes, you need time to bond but they still need their "mommy" or "daddy" time. They need

to know they still have the relationship with their parent, even though this new intruder is in their life.

REFLECTION QUESTIONS

1. Were you familiar with the term "loyalty bind?" Do you think that your stepchildren may feel a loyalty bind sometimes?

2. WHICH OF THESE THINGS ARE YOU ALREADY DOING, TO connect with your stepchild(ren)?
   a. Listening
   b. Doing stuff together
   c. Honouring both of their parents

3. WHICH OF THE FOLLOWING THINGS (IF ANY) DO YOU NEED TO work on, regarding connecting with your stepchild(ren)?
   a. Listening
   b. Doing stuff together
   c. Honouring both of their parents

VI

TAKING CARE OF YOURSELF

This part of the book deals with taking care of yourself, amidst all the craziness of a second marriage. We examine the importance of maintaining your own life and identity within the marriage.

19

DON'T FORGET WHO YOU ARE

 To thine own self be true.

— WILLIAM SHAKESPEARE

*A*ngus Jones credits his Harley Davidson for keeping him sane during the stress he experienced from conflict with his ex-wife. He says, "I think every one of the men reading this book should go out and buy himself a Harley."

Not all of us can go and buy a Harley (or would want to) but we need to find our own ways of keeping our identity, especially when the pressure is on. You need to have things in your life that are separate from being a wife, or a husband, and are just "you."

Whether it's going jogging, going out with a friend, playing a computer game, or knitting, don't lose your identity! Maintaining yourself as an individual is as important as learning to become a couple.

Being "you' will help you navigate the challenging times and remind you that you are a valuable person, regardless of what is happening in your marriage and stepfamily. Doing things on your own will remind you of your identity before you became a wife or a husband.

You probably already know that you must fight for this time alone. It won't come easy. You may have to battle your own guilt and overwhelm. It will likely be difficult to make room in your schedule and your partner may not fully understand, but in spite of all of these difficulties, having some time to do what you enjoy will be worth it.

BEING YOURSELF STRENGTHENS YOUR MARRIAGE

Let's consider Rachel Marten's situation from the previous chapter. She felt very overwhelmed when, at 28-year old years old, she suddenly became a full-time mother to a seventeen-year-old teenage boy and two daughters, aged ten and eleven.

What helped Rachel was getting into self-help books. "I read so many books that helped me with being okay with myself." As she started to read these books, she felt stronger in who she was and this helped her marriage. Rachel says that she learned to stand up for herself when her husband hurt her feelings.

 I had to learn to accept myself. He would hurt me but I would stay strong. I was good at it. I wouldn't go to him right away. I knew he would come to me. I knew it would be okay.

When we strengthen the essence of who we are, we have more to bring to the relationship. We are not ripped apart when we have an agreement with our spouse. We can be strong enough to endure the ups and downs.

We are less dependent on the marriage to bolster our own insecurities and fears. As we become stronger, our spouse will notice it, even subconsciously, and start to realize that they can no longer push the same buttons that they used to, and we will gain their respect.

BUILD YOUR FAITH

Part of becoming stronger is to build your faith. In the movie, *War Room*,[1] Elizabeth Jordan's spouse comes very close to having an affair. Her best friend sees her husband with another woman and sends Elizabeth a text to let her know that it appears her spouse may be cheating on her.

This sends her into a tailspin and she breaks down and cries out to God. "Please don't let him do this, God. Make our marriage strong again, O LORD. Save our marriage" This crisis event triggers a barrage of continual fervent prayer to God concerning her marriage. As she prays, she begins to see her own heart and starts to change her behaviour.

Her husband also sees a change in her and feels confused by what is happening to his wife. In one humorous scene, he finds out that his wife knows about the affair. She acts super-nice to him and he thinks she is trying to mess with his head and he looks at her suspiciously, just waiting for her to lash out at him but she never does.

Her faith has made her stronger within herself and with

God and this alone changes the whole dynamic of the marriage.

As I have alluded to throughout the book, I am a person of faith. I am a Christian and my faith has helped me get through the hardest times of my life, including the trials of second marriage.

If you are a person of faith, I encourage you to look to God. A time of hardship can push us to really examine what we believe and we can learn to trust God in a new way. Look to the Scripture for help. Pray. Get support from those who also believe.

The Bible says that God will be with us in the worst of our circumstances and through them, we will become purer and more refined. Trust that this will make you stronger and that He is with you.

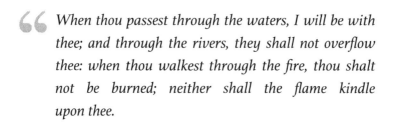

When thou passest through the waters, I will be with thee; and through the rivers, they shall not overflow thee: when thou walkest through the fire, thou shalt not be burned; neither shall the flame kindle upon thee.

— ISAIAH 43:2

TAKE CARE OF YOUR OWN NEEDS, TOO

Betty Jones is a very nurturing individual. She teaches Sunday School, reaches out to her elderly neighbours and dotes on her grandchildren. Even her job as a kindergarten teacher involves worrying about the needs of others who depend on her. What Betty has realized over the years, though, is the importance of taking care of her own needs, too. She shares, "Lots of things I do will please him. I do that but you also need a balance. It's important to meet my own needs, too."

Part of meeting your own needs is taking time to do something that you really enjoy. During our second year of marriage, when the pressure seemed to be the worst, is when I started some online hobbies. One was a program called Polyvore. The other was a humble blog that eventually led me to pursue my current path of full-time writer.

These were *my* interests. At the time, my husband had no interest in these activities and openly questioned why I was wasting time on the computer, when there was so much to do.

But those few hours a week were my lifeline. I was dealing with a stressful career as a teacher, being a part-time Mom to two teenagers and a new marriage that was rife with conflict. I needed some time to just "be me."

Another part of taking care of your own needs is understanding your personality needs. If you are an introvert, you will need some time to yourself. If you are an extrovert, you will need some friends time. These are things you need in order to function properly and not just frivolous desires.

Taking care of your own needs also means that you take care of your body, as in getting enough sleep and making food choices that give you energy to keep going.

It is not an easy balance to include ourselves on the list of people that we worry about but it is important. Just remember that if you are married, part of staying married is remembering the "you" in "you and me."

REFLECTION QUESTIONS

1. Do you ever feel like you are losing sight of who *you* are, within your marriage?

2. WHAT ACTIVITIES OR PURSUITS DO YOU HAVE IN YOUR LIFE that remind you that you are still "you?"

20

WHEN YOU FEEL LONELY

66 Walking with a friend in the dark is better than walking alone in the light.

— HELEN KELLER

*D*o you feel like you are the only one in the world who is going through this? Does it seem like no one could ever relate? Trust me when I say that you are far from alone, but I know that sometimes it sure feels like it.

In 2014, approximately 2.1 million couples got married in the United States.[1] About 40% of those marriages were remarriages, which is about 840,000 marriages.[2] Let's break that down even further. This means that on average, every week, there are roughly 16,000 couples entering a second marriage in the U.S.A. alone.

There are a lot of us out here but we still feel alone. During the first few years of my second marriage, I felt like I was the only one in the world who had these kinds of struggles.

I knew of no one in my circles who could relate to what I was going through. I didn't even know how to communicate all that I was experiencing. It felt like no one would ever understand.

When I started my book, and told people what it was about, an interesting thing happened. Several people came up and told me they were in a second marriage. I had no idea they had been married before! Even more surprisingly, they wanted to talk to me about their situation. What I learned from that experience was that I was not nearly as alone as I thought I was.

Take hope in the fact that you are not alone in your situation. There are many out there just like us. I encourage you to start believing that you are not the only one and start looking for some "second marriage kindred spirits." You may be surprised at who you find.

Try sending out a few feelers with the people that you already know at work, church, or within your other circles. There may be people in second marriages that haven't shared that part of their life with you. To get them to open up, you could share a little bit of your life, mentioning a little story that happened with your stepchild, for example. If they also have stepchildren, they may share in return.

STEPFAMILIES CAN BE LONELY

When Rachel Martens came to Canada from Greece to marry John, she felt very lonely. She had just come from another country, far from family and friends and was spending her time as a full-time mother to children that didn't even know her. It is completely understandable that she felt lonely in this situation.

Maybe you can relate to Rachel. It is ironic that we marry to gain companionship but second marriage can make us even lonelier. The newly formed stepfamily can be a source of loneliness for all those involved. Unlike the Brady Bunch, we don't automatically become one big happy family.

Children and stepparents can take a long time to feel comfortable with one another. If there are two sets of children (one from each spouse) it is even more challenging, as stepbrothers and sisters must learn to get along with each other, and also share their parents with other children.

People in this new blended family can feel lonely because they don't feel connected to their new family members. They may feel left out by their non-biological family members, not intentionally, but because the biological members have known each other for longer.

If you are a stepmom or dad, you may feel lonely when you are not able to connect with your step kids. You can also feel left out of the close relationship that the biological parent has with her children. It's nobody's fault but it a result of trying to form a family out of people that don't know each other that well.

In the first few years of a second marriage, it is also very common to have disagreements about how to handle the children and these arguments can make you feel even more lonely.

If you are feeling loneliness because of the dynamics in your stepfamily, please be assured that is normal and will get better in time, as you all get to know one another better and feel more comfortable together.

WE SOMETIMES FEEL STIGMATIZED

When my husband and I first got married, we were eager to get into a church to share and grow in our faith. We ended up moving back into the community where my husband and his ex-wife had lived years earlier.

I was concerned that church members might feel uncomfortable with us because they had known Vern with his ex-wife. My husband assured me that this would not be an issue because the people at this church were very supportive and understanding.

One Sunday, one of the ladies of the church came up and told me that she had really liked my husband's ex-wife and she wasn't sure of how she felt about *me* being with him. When she told me this, I was stunned. I thanked her for telling me that, but afterwards, I felt kind of numb.

I don't know if she was, but it seemed like she had been watching and judging me. Even though both of us had been left by our spouses and had met years later, I felt a sort of stigma was put on me. I know I am not the only one who has felt this way, as a person in a remarriage.

In fact, research has found that society, in general, still puts a stigma on those in stepfamily situations. In their book, *Stepfamily Relationships: Development, Dynamics and Interventions*, Lawrence Gagnon and Marilyn Coleman observe that stepfamilies tend to hide the truth from strangers about their struggles because they feel an unspoken stigma from those around them.[3]

Gagnon and Coleman found that there was even a prejudice from people in the caregiving professions toward stepfamilies.[4] People around us may not understand and that can make us feel a bit hesitant to talk about our situation when we need the support the most.

LOOK FOR SUPPORT

Even though it may be intimidating, it is important to find support. If you don't have anyone in your circles, check out your community. Although they are not that common, some universities, churches and community centres offer support groups for stepfamilies. As well, you can go online and see if you can find something that suits you. Here are a few ideas for online second marriage / stepfamily supports:

a. **Meet Up**: This is a site where you can find groups that meet up on many different topics, and I have seen some on stepfamilies. This site has groups for cities across North America. You will have to check it to see if there are any groups in your area.

b. **Stepmoms on a Mission**: This is a group I tried and it seemed supportive. It is specifically for stepmoms.

c. **Second Chance Love**: This is the Facebook page that I run. We put out links to encourage those in second marriage.

I also hope that you will feel less alone as you read about the stories from the couples in this book, all who have gone through struggles in their marriage, possibly some of the same struggles that you may be going through now.

For more books, websites and services on the topic of second marriage and stepfamilies, check out the Recommended Resources section at the end of the book. You can also check out the Recommended Resources section of my website, *Second Chance Love*, where I feature a short review of all the materials and sites that I endorse. The link to that page is here:

http://secondmarriage.xyz/recommended-resources8587

DON'T ISOLATE YOURSELF FROM LOVED ONES

Sometimes when we enter a second marriage, we feel so overwhelmed by the situation that we isolate ourselves from other people, not wanting them to find out about the mess we seem to have found ourselves in. We may also be nervous about whether our family will be supportive. When Elise Roca was going through some of the roughest times in her marriage, she tried to tell her mother but says, "My Mom would tell me, "Why do you put up with him?""

Right now, you probably need support more than at any time of your life, so make sure that you don't cut yourself off from friends and family. Make sure that you keep in touch with those who love you: "your people." Even if you can't talk to them in detail about your situation, they are the ones that know you the best and you need them. Don't let embarrassment about your situation keep you isolated.

REACH OUT TO OTHERS

During my first marriage, I told a friend of mine that I was feeling depressed. She told me that the best way to get out of a funk was to help someone else. And I want to share her advice, a bit modified, with you today. It might sound counterintuitive, but one of the best antidotes to loneliness is to reach out to someone else.

Let me share a story with you. About six years ago, on Mother's Day, I was feeling sorry for myself. Of course, the boys were with their mother on this day and I felt left out.

My husband was working all weekend and even though I made meals, gave talks and constantly worried about the boys, I was not considered a mother by the children that consumed so much of my life. On top of all that, I felt sad that my own mother had passed away.

I was sitting in my house when I heard a knock on the door. Now, in our neighbourhood, at the time, many of us didn't answer the door because it was usually a solicitor. I listened to the knock but did not go to answer it. When I went to check to see if the person had gone away, I was so amazed!

Inside the mailbox was a small red card that read "Happy Mother's Day." Our next-door neighbour, a sweet, eccentric older lady named Rose, had taken the time to reach out and give me a card on Mother's Day, acknowledging my difficult position as a stepmother. She knew and understood my feelings because she was a stepmother, too, with grown-up children.

I can't emphasize enough how much that little card meant to me. It felt like no one saw me and no one understood. But that sweet little elderly lady, who I am sure was lonely herself, reached out to me on that sad day and made a dramatic difference to me. I don't know about you but this really inspires me!

When we feel lonely, one of the most powerful ways that we can break through our loneliness is to reach out to someone else. That someone else may be even lonelier than we are.

We can send a little card or ask to visit them for half an hour. Sometimes it might be a phone call or connecting on Facebook. A smile or a short conversation with someone can be a way of reaching out. The important thing is that when we get our minds off ourselves for a little while and see someone else, we will be blessed in return!

"I'M SO LONELY" EXERCISE

Sometime in the next week, phone, write an e-mail, text or connect on Facebook with someone that you haven't spoken to in a while. This could be a friend, family member or former colleague.

Lightly share a bit about your life and listen to what is happening with them. If they are in your city or town and you feel comfortable doing so, invite them for coffee or some other event.

21

GETTING SOME HELP

> To listen well, is as powerful a means of influence as to talk well, and is as essential to all true conversation..

— CHINESE PROVERB

*A*s we have discussed throughout this book, second marriage is more difficult and often more complicated than marriage the first time around. There are special challenges that we deal with that make it harder to maintain connections and keep our relationship strong. Sometimes we need to talk to someone in person who can help us sort out the issues that keep coming up and threatening our relationship.

Getting help with your relationship can one of the best decisions you make to help build your life together as a couple. In this next section, I will share the story of how marriage counselling helped to save our marriage. If you are in a similar situation, you may want to consider counselling as an option.

MARRIAGE COUNSELLING SAVED OUR MARRIAGE

Three years into our marriage, my husband and I argued constantly, and didn't know how to stop. My husband was mean: like a street fighter with his words – he aimed to hurt me, and he did. I was like a little girl who got her feelings hurt at almost everything that he said. I became very distraught and then I would yell back, at the top of my lungs. In fact, I would yell so loud that I would lose my voice.

On one particular night, my husband got so angry with me, he yelled at me to "get out." It made me feel like a dog. I ran to the car in complete hysterics, sobbing at the top of my lungs. I don't remember what we were fighting about but it was usually about housework, or the kids. Sometimes it was my raving jealousy.

Weeping in the car, I started driving towards the home of our elders in the church, who lived about two miles down the road. I arrived at their doorstop in tears, completely dishevelled. The man of the house, a dear elder from the church who had known Vern for years, went over to our house and talked to Vern, asking him to come over so we could all talk.

Meanwhile, I sat and spoke with his dear wife who offered me some coffee and tried to calm me down. When my husband came in the house, I had no desire to speak with him, but this wonderful, sweet couple stopped whatever they were doing that night and listened to both of us. My husband tried to joke his way out of it and I couldn't finish a sentence without sobbing.

We talked for a little while, with a promise for another appointment with them later that week. We both went home, barely talking and spent an icy night in bed, backs turned, completely separated. I did not want to be married to him at this point.

Later that week, we spent some time at this couples' place and they tried again to bring us to reason. But we were just too far gone at that point. Seeing our sad state, this couple did something amazing for us: they suggested that we try marriage counselling. They gave us two names and we took one of them.

A few weeks later, we decided to actually go to the counselling. I don't remember exactly what we talked about in the first session, but I do remember feeling some hope that we might be able to solve what was happening between us.

At first, it was very rocky. I was crying a lot. My husband felt like he was getting picked on. It didn't seem like it was helping all that much. But we persisted, not knowing what else to do. And slowly, we started to listen to one another and understand each other.

In time, therapy helped us both understand the root of our anger. It took a long time, but my husband realized that his resentment came from childhood.

He had been taken from his family home as a baby and never returned in the infamous 60's scoop. He was then passed around from foster home to foster home, until he was adopted into another family. This was all done without the consent of his biological mother, who fought to get him back but the courts refused.

Even though my husband was just a baby at the time, it affected him deeply. The therapist said he had something called "attachment disorder" which made it hard for him to get close to other people. As he and the counsellor worked through these deep issues, his heart started to heal from these very profound hurts.

In the meantime, I needed to work on my own anger issues. I was so quick to get angry and retaliate back at Vern when we were fighting. I always blamed him but had a difficult time looking at my self.

I also had childhood issues that needed to be resolved. I had been brought up in an abusive home and witnessed and heard verbal and emotional abuse.

I remember feeling very helpless to do anything, but as I got older I also became an angry person. In my marriage, that anger came out as defensiveness and I would retaliate fiercely when my husband got angry with me.

The marriage counselling took two full years of working through our issues, and how our words affected each other. He was verbally abusive to me and at first, he couldn't see what an impact his words were having on me.

Then during one session, our counsellor finally got through to him. Vern had said something to me that was hurtful and damaging. I had told her what he had said and she was concerned for me. She tried talking to him but he got so mad that he left the session and started walking the two hours towards our home.

I stayed and talked to her and she said that she supported

me leaving my husband, if things did not change. I left the session and started driving towards our home, when I saw my husband on the walking trail going home. I stopped the car and he got in, and he seemed like a different man. His face was humbled. He said he was sorry and he saw it had been wrong to talk to me like that.

When our marriage was on the brink of destruction, we were both hurting, angry people but our skilled counsellor helped us discover the love that was hiding underneath all the hurt and anger. Our counselling went on for over two years, but it was worth the money, the time, and the work. It took a long time because of the complexity we were dealing with. This was our story. If you are at a crisis point in your marriage, counselling is something to consider.

YOU MIGHT NEED MARRIAGE COUNSELLING IF ...

I believe that the right kind of marriage counselling *can* save a marriage because it gives you the tools to make changes and a place to heal. If you are on the fence about marriage counselling, this is a list of six reasons why it might be right for you.

You might need marriage counselling if:

1. You need to break the logjam between you.

If you can't seem to ever stop arguing, and the fights have been going on for weeks, months or even years, it sounds like you need a third party to intervene.

2. You haven't been able to heal from your past, on your own.

If you and/or your partner have not been able to heal from

events in your history, even though you have tried on your own, it might be time to get some outside assistance.

3. Your children are being affected by the conflict.

If you have kids, your children are being affected by the tension in your relationship, and they also deserve to have more peace in their home.

4. You are having serious problems with communication.

If you and your partner find it difficult to talk to one another, some good counselling can help you learn strategies for better communication. It will also give both of you an opportunity to have the floor and let the other person know what you need.

5. You want to invest in your marriage.

Even if you are not having serious problems in your marriage, a counsellor can still assist you in making things better. Any kind of marriage training can help make your relationship even better.

6. You are dealing with adultery, addictions or abuse.

If you are dealing with any of these "three A's," I urge you to get professional help. Even if it is not a counsellor, talk to someone you trust about what you are going through.

HOW TO FIND A MARRIAGE COUNSELLOR

Our counsellor was so good that I wish everyone could go to her. If anyone lives in my area, I would highly recommend her! Obviously, though, not everyone will be able to go to our counsellor, so this next section offers some tips for finding a skilled professional to help you.

My first suggestion is to look for referrals from people you know. This way, someone you trust will be making the recommendation. This is a far more reliable source than choosing a random person.

This could be potentially awkward, because most of us don't share with our friends that we are having marriage difficulties. But if you feel comfortable, try asking someone that you think might know. It might be an older couple that you respect or friends that you suspect are having marriage problems.

Another source of referrals can be your church or faith group. Some churches have pastors that offer counselling. This can be a good place to start, but please be aware that not all pastors are qualified or really devoted to counselling. Some may have that gifting, and if they do, that is a real blessing.

Some churches also have a qualified counsellor on staff, or a list of counsellors that they recommend. Even if you are not a member of the church, they will usually be glad to offer some referrals.

There are also many secular organizations that offer counselling for the community. These organizations tend to take longer to get into but their prices are usually scaled for income, if you are looking for something more affordable.

Finally, you can start looking up counsellors online. Look for ones that appeal to you and seem to have a philosophy that suits you.

WHAT TO LOOK FOR IN A COUNSELLOR

Once you have found a counsellor, I would recommend going for a testing session first, to see if it is a good fit. Not all counsellors will be suitable for you and your spouse. Find someone that you feel comfortable talking with, not someone that makes you feel pressured or uneasy.

Don't feel bad if it isn't a fit for your personalities. You must be able to fully trust this person in order to do the challenging work that therapeutic work entails.

Try to find someone that has similar values to you. If you are a person of faith and want to discuss faith issues in your sessions, it is important to find someone that respects your beliefs. They might not have the exact same beliefs as you but they should be open to and respectful towards your values.

For this chapter's exercise, I will give you a list that can help you screen a marriage counsellor. If you are still not sure, take some time to think about it. It is better to be sure than to rush into counselling that is not comfortable for you.

QUESTIONS

This is a list of questions you can ask a marriage counsellor before you start. Many therapists will offer a free half-hour session to see if it is a good fit.

1. WHAT KIND OF APPROACH DO YOU TAKE TO COUNSELLING? (IF they say something but you don't understand the term, ask them to explain.)

2. IF YOU ARE A PERSON OF FAITH, ASK THE FOLLOWING QUESTION: What is your view of (whatever your faith is)?

· · ·

3. How would we decide what to talk about?

4. What would our goals be for the therapy?

5. What is your professional background?

6. What do you like about the job of counselling?

22

CONCLUSION

*D*uring my first year of marriage, I started looking for answers. Would this get any easier? I wondered. The best book I could find that related to my situation was called *Smart Stepfamilies: Seven Steps to a Better Family.* The author, Ron Deal, states that, according to research, it takes an average of *five to seven years* for a blended family to come together after remarriage.[1]

When I read this statistic, I didn't believe it and thought it must be an exaggeration. Even though the book gave example after example of this truth born out in people's lives, I refused to believe that it would take that long. I wanted it to be a much quicker process.

Can you relate? We don't want to have to wait for our families to come together but we must remember that it can be a long process. Don't expect it to happen overnight. This is definitely not the Brady Bunch.

To close this section, I am going to share a little story that illustrates why I do not find that seven-year statistic so hard to believe anymore.

About two years ago, my husband and I were walking down the beach with his two sons. It was a crisp autumn evening and the wind was blowing on the lake, creating ferocious waves. We had not seen the boys in a few months and prior to that, the relationship had gone through a rocky time.

We were walking, all smiling at one another. The boys told us they were grateful to us for helping them in a recent crisis. The youngest boy was smiling at me with affection. I smiled back. There was no awkward distance between us. I knew that I loved them and believe they knew it, too. We were all relaxed.

As we all walked, enjoying the waves and the beauty of the beach, I remembered that book I had read during the first year of marriage. I recalled reading about that seven-year statistic and how annoyed I had felt when I first read it.

But here it was, I realized, almost exactly seven years after our wedding, and it *finally* felt like we were a family. But it *really had* taken seven years to get here! Seven years that were, at times, agonizing. There were many times when I wanted to walk away and never talk to any of them again. Times when it seemed beyond impossible that it would ever get better.

But now, we were all getting along. The relationships were comfortable. My husband and I were getting along, too. Things felt normal.

And so, I encourage you once again. If you are in a second marriage that seems impossible right now, there is hope. If you are struggling with stepfamily issues that feel like they will never be resolved, be patient. Remember that many stepfamilies take five to seven years to become stabilized. Even if you are in a second marriage without kids, there can still be issues from your past that must be worked out. This can take a long time, so resolve to have your eye on the end game.

SOME PARTING ADVICE

As I wrote this book, I talked to several people in second marriages, both through an online survey, through the interviews and simply sharing with friends who were in a second marriage. Almost everyone I spoke with said: "Hold on. It gets better."

At the end of the interviews, I asked them for some advice they would give to someone struggling in their second marriage. I would like to share their words with you:

RACHEL SAYS:

Pray! If you love each other and are committed, trust that it will work out. It will get better.

BETTY SAYS THIS:

Talk to people who have been through it. Ask them, "What was it like for you?" And you should probably seek counselling before it gets to the point of causing a lot of problems.

ANGUS SAYS:

Both parties have to be open to meeting half way.

· · ·

ELISE TELLS US:

The main important thing is not to give up when you love someone. I made a vow to God and I won't break up. There is hope for your future and for your family!

MARIA SAYS:

Talk. Never assume your partner knows what you need, think, feel or believe. Assume that the goal of your relationship is to help both of you live the most fulfilling lives you can.

EPILOGUE

> *To everything there is a season, and a time to every purpose under the heaven ... A time to weep, and a time to laugh; a time to mourn, and a time to dance.*
> *Ecclesiastes 3:1, 4*

Would you dare to believe ... that all your heartache will some day turn into the unspeakable joy of having endured to the end?

WOULD YOU DARE TO BELIEVE ... THAT YOUR CONSTANT FIGHTING will eventually transform into a marriage that has transcended a thousand struggles and prevailed?

WOULD YOU DARE TO BELIEVE ... THAT THE CHILDREN WHO ARE

hurting so much now, from all the changes, will someday know you did everything you could to make their lives better?

DO YOU DARE TO BELIEVE ... THAT THE SORROW OF LOSING YOUR first spouse has brought you another spouse who will comfort you in your old age?

DO YOU DARE TO BELIEVE ... THAT YOUR TIME OF MOURNING IS over and now it is time to dance?

DO YOU DARE TO BELIEVE ... THAT THE SEEDS OF UNSELFISHNESS you plant today will bloom into beautiful blossoms of a love that cannot be broken?

REMEMBER THAT ... LOVE IS AS STRONG AS DEATH. EVEN A flood cannot drown love.

> *Set me as a seal upon thine heart, as a seal upon thine arm: for love is strong as death; jealousy is cruel as the grave ... Many waters cannot quench love, neither can the floods drown it.*

> — SONG OF SOLOMON 8: 6A, 7A

THANK YOU

Thank you *so* much for sharing this journey with me! I pray it has given you hope, and some practical strategies for staying the course. May your second marriage truly be full of hope, healing and love!

I have just one favour to ask. If you loved the book, would you spend a few minutes to help to spread the word by leaving a review on Amazon, or another place, such as Goodreads?

When you leave a review, it helps spread this message of encouragement to the world. Reviews are the number one way that writers get a good reputation, and are able to keep doing what they love: writing more books.

ABOUT THE AUTHOR

Sharilee Swaity has a strong academic interest in the subject of relationships. During her ten years of classroom experience, Sharilee witnessed first-hand the effects of divorce and family breakdowns on children and families.

Sharilee has a Bachelor of Education from the University of Calgary and a lifelong interest in human relationship books and materials.

Sharilee and her husband, Vern are both in their second marriage and live in the woods of Central Canada. She has helped her husband raise two now-grown sons. They share their home with three cats and occasionally witness a bear on their deck.

She can be followed at:

[f] facebook.com/secondmarriagetransformed

[Instagram] instagram.com/lifeinwoods

RECOMMENDED RESOURCES

I have compiled a list of marriage resources that I personally recommend. This means that I either have personal experience with them or have reviewed them thoroughly. For a more detailed review, go to this page for a linked list, with a small review about each item:

http://secondmarriage.xyz/recommended-resources8587

RECOMMENDED BOOKS

Books about Second Marriage

The Heart of Remarriage, by Gary Smalley

Successful Second Marriages, by Patricia Bubash, M.Ed.

Saving Your Second Marriage Before It Starts: Nine Questions to

Ask Before – and After – You Remarry, by Drs. Les and Leslie Parrot

Books About Being a Stepparent

131 Conversations for Stepfamily Success: How to Grow Intimacy, Parent as a Team and Build a Joyful Home (Creative Conversations Series Book 6), by Jed Jurchenko

The Smart Stepfamily: Seven Steps to a Happy Family, by Ron Deal

StepMonster: A New Look at Why Real Stepmothers Think, Feel, and Act the Way They Do, by Wednesday Martin

Wisdom on Stepparenting: How to Succeed Where Others Fail, by Diane Weiss-Wisdom

General Marriage Books

The Mystery of Marriage: Meditations on the Miracle, by Mike Mason

The Five Love Languages, by Gary Chapman

Seven Principles for Making Marriage Work: A Practical Guide from the Country's Foremost Relationship Expert, by John Gottman

Love and Respect: The Love She Most Desires and the Respect He Desperately Needs, by Emmerson Eggerichs

Books About Tough Issues in Marriage

The Verbally Abusive Relationship, Expanded Third Edition: How to Recognize It and How to Respond, by Patricia Evans

Love Must Be Tough: New Hope for Marriages in Crisis, by James Dobson

Why Does He Do That?: Inside the Minds of Controlling and Angry Men, by Lundy Bancroft

WEBSITES

Websites About Second Marriage

Second Chance Love: (This is my own personal blog on second marriage): http://secondmarriage.xyz

Second Chance Love Facebook Page: https://www.facebook.com/secondmarriagetransformed/. This is the Facebook page I run about Second Marriage

Websites About Being a Stepparent

Smart Stepfamilies: http://www.smartstepfamilies.com. This site is run by Ron Deal, one of the world's foremost experts on stepfamilies.

Step Mother Support: http://www.stepmothersupport.com. This site offers a lot of in-depth support for stepmoms.

Stepmom Mag: http://www.stepmothersupport.com. This online magazine offers great content on stepparenting issues.

Websites About Marriage in General

To Love, Honor and Vacuum: http://tolovehonorandvacuum.com. This is a website targeted at women offering humour and wisdom for handling marriage.

One Flesh Marriage: https://www.onefleshmarriage.com. This site offers frank, encouraging advice for married Christians who want to honour Christ in their relationship.

Family Life Today: http://www.familylife.com. A comprehensive site to help you in all aspects of your marriage.

Marriage Training Websites

Prepare -Enrich: https://www.prepare-enrich.com. This site offers a test that will help you pinpoint weaknesses and strengths in your marriage.

E-Prep: https://www.lovetakeslearning.com. This site offers training online to deal with common marriage issues.

NOTES

ABOUT THIS BOOK

1. "Ten Tips for a Happy Second Marriage" https://pairedlife.com/relationships/Tips-for-Staying-Together-in-a-Second-Marriage

1. WE DON'T WANT TO MARRY AGAIN BUT...

1. Pascale Beau. 2008. *I do-- take two: changes in intentions to remarry among divorced Canadians during the past 20 years.* Ottawa, Ontario: Statistics Canada, General Social Survey, 2008. Accessed 02 12, 2017. http://www.statcan.gc.ca/pub/89-630-x/2008001/article/10659-eng.htm
2. Coleman, M., Ganong, L., & Fine, M. 2000. "Reinvestigating Remarriage: Another Decade of Progress." *Journal of Marriage and Family.* Accessed February 2017, 14. https://libres.uncg.edu/ir/uncg/f/M_Fine_Reinvestigating_2000.pdf
3. Pew Research Center 2014. "Four-in-Ten Couples are Saying "I Do," Again." Washington, D.C. Accessed Feburary 12, 2017. http://www.pewsocialtrends.org/2014/11/14/four-in-ten-couples-are-saying-i-do-again

2. MOST OF US REMARRY QUICKLY

1. Coleman, M., Ganong, L., & Fine, M. 2000. "Reinvestigating Remarriage: Another Decade of Progress." *Journal of Marriage and Family.* Accessed February 2017. https://libres.uncg.edu/ir/uncg/f/M_Fine_Reinvestigating_2000.pdf

3. WHY ARE THINGS SO COMPLICATED?

1. Hammond, R., Cheney, P, Pearsey, R. 2015. "Sociology of the Family."
2. McKenna, Aline Brosh and Mee, Benjamin. 2011. *We Bought A Zoo*. Directed by Cameron Crowe. Produced by 20th Century Fox Home Entertainment.

4. COMPLICATED EMOTIONS

1. Conkie, H. (Writer) and Potter, C. (Director). 2010. "The Happy Life." *Heartland*. Seven24 Films, watched on NetFlix. Accessed February 18, 2017.

6. WHY IS IT SO HARD TO LET GO?

1. Hammond, R., Cheney, P, Pearsey, R. 2015. "Sociology of the Family." Accessed February 18, 2017. http://freesociologybooks.com/Sociology_Of_The_Family
2. "The Holmes-Rahe Stress Inventory." *The American Institute of Stress*. Accessed February 17, 2017. http://www.stress.org/holmes-rahe-stress-inventory/.
3. Zisook, S., Chentsova-Dutton, Y. & Shuchter, S.R. 1998. "PTSD Following Bereavement." *Annals of Clincal Psychiatry* 10 (157). Accessed February 23, 2017. https://sites.duke.edu/flaubertsbrain/files/2012/08/Chentsova-Dutton-PTSD-Following-Bereavement.pdf.
4. Arends, Lisa. n.d. *Lessons From the End of a Marriage -- About*. Accessed February 24, 2017. https://lessonsfromtheendofamarriage.com/about/.
5. Arends, Lisa. 2013. *PTSD After Divorce*. January 2013. Accessed February 24, 2017. http://www.huffingtonpost.com/lisa-arends/ptsd-after-divorce_b_2519897.html.
6. *Posttraumatic Stress Disorder*. Accessed Feburary 23, 2017. http://traumadissociation.com/ptsd.html.
7. Need to find source for this one!

9. FORGIVENESS

1. **Chapter 10 Notes**
   Leaf, Dr. Caroline. 2013. *Switch Your Brain: The Key to Peak Happiness, Thinking, and Health, pg. 72*. Ada, MI: Baker Books. Accessed March 7, 2017, via Kindle.

10. WHEN YOU FEEL INSECURE

1. Beatty, Roger (writer) and Powers,Dave (director). 1977. "Wrong Number, from Family." *Carol Burnett and Friends.* Inc, Whacko. Beverley Hills, CA, January 22. Accessed March 10, 2017, via Youtube. https://www.youtube.com/watch?v=vpSk2Hvqqgk.

12. ARE WE DESTINED FOR LOVE?

1. Acevedo, Bianca, Aron, Arthur, Fisher, Helen E. and Brown, Lucy L. 2012. "Neural correlates of long-term intense romantic love." *Social, Cognitive and Affective Neuroscience* 7 (2): 145-159. Accessed March 22, 2017. https://academic.oup.com/scan/article/7/2/145/1622197#

2. Aron, Arthur and Melinat, Edward and Aron, Elaine N, Vallone, Robert Darrin and Bator, Renee J. 1997."The Experimental Generation of Interpersonal Closeness: A Procedure and some Preliminary Findings." *Personal and Social Psychology Bulletin* 23 (4): 363-377. Accessed March 22, 2017. http://journals.sagepub.com/doi/pdf/10.1177/0146167297234003.

3. Carton, Mandy Len. 2015. "To Fall in Love With Anyone, Do This." *New York Times* . January 9. Accessed March 22, 2017. https://www.nytimes.com/2015/01/11/fashion/modern-love-to-fall-in-love-with-anyone-do-this.html

4. Soul Pancake. 2015. "How to Connect With Anyone." February 12, via Youtube. Accessed 23 2017, March . https://www.youtube.com/watch?v=Xm-T3HCa618

13. TO KNOW YOU IS TO LOVE YOU

1. Nicholson, Nick. 1966-1977. *The Newlywed Game.* Chuck Barriss Productions

2. 2017. *Strong's H3045 - yada.* Accessed March 23, 2017. https://www.blueletterbible.org/lang/Lexicon/Lexicon.cfm?strongs=H3045&t=KJV

3. Zakicha, Rhea. n.d. "The Ungame." *1972.* Accessed March 26, 2017. http://rheazakich.com/wp/?page_id=34

4. Clarke, Cristy. n.d. "TableTopics." Commerce. http://www.tabletopics.com/about_us/

5. Fleiss, Mike (producer) 2002-2017. "The Bachelor." Next Entertainment

14. YOU'RE MY BEST FRIEND

1. Parker, Robyn. 2004. *Why Marriages Last: A Discussion of the Literature* . Research Paper, Melbourne: Australian Institute of Family Studies. Accessed March 28, 2017. https://aifs.gov.au/publications/why-marriages-last/studies-lasting-marriages.

16. THE DANCE OF OPPOSITES

1. Jung, Carl, 1971. *Psychological Types, Collected Works of C.G. Jung*
2. Glenna Stacer-Sayles (producer) 2013-2017. *Fixer Upper,* High Noon Entertainment, Waco, Texas

17. BECOMING A FAMILY

1. **Chapter 18 Notes**
Coleman, M., Ganong, L., & Fine, M. 2000. "Reinvestigating Remarriage: Another Decade of Progress." *Journal of Marriage and Family.* Accessed February 2017, 14. https://libres.uncg.edu/ir/uncg/f/M_Fine_Reinvestigating_2000.pdf

19. DON'T FORGET WHO YOU ARE

1. Kendrick, Alex 2015. *War Room.* Faith Step Films, Albany, Georgia.

20. WHEN YOU FEEL LONELY

1. National Center for Health Statistics. Marriage and Divorce. Accessed February 22, 2017. https://www.cdc.gov/nchs/fastats/marriage-divorce.htm. (National Center for Health Statistics n.d.)
2. Pew Research Center 2014. "Four-in-Ten Couples are Saying "I Do," Again." Washington, D.C. Accessed Feburary 12, 2017. http://www.pewsocialtrends.org/2014/11/14/four-in-ten-couples-are-saying-i-do-again/
3. Gangong Lawrence and Coleman, Marilyn. 2016. *Stepfamily Relationships: Development, Dynamics and Interventions.* New York City, pg 2: Springer.

Accessed   March   14,   2017.   https://books.google.ca/books?
id=H16vDAAAQBAJ&source=gbs_navlinks_s
4. (Gangong 2016)

22. CONCLUSION

1. Deal, Ron 2002. *The Smart Stepfamily: Seven Steps to a Healthy Family*, pg.
40. Bethany House Publishers.

Made in the USA
San Bernardino, CA
04 January 2019